DESIGN
YOUR OWN
WEBSITE

This is a **FLAME TREE** book
First published 2010

Publisher and Creative Director: Nick Wells
Project Editor and Picture Research: Catherine Taylor
Editorial and Picture Research: Sonya Newland
Art Director: Mike Spender
Layout Design: Dave Jones
Digital Design and Production: Chris Herbert
Proofreader: Dawn Laker
Indexer: Helen Snaith

Special thanks to Rhys Lewis for additional help and contributions.

This edition first published 2010 by
FLAME TREE PUBLISHING
Crabtree Hall, Crabtree Lane
Fulham, London SW6 6TY
United Kingdom

www.flametreepublishing.com

14
5 7 9 10 8 6 4

ISBN 978-1-84786-707-0

A CIP record for this book is available from the British Library upon request.

Printed in China

All pictures are courtesy of Foundry Arts or Rhys Lewis, except the following, which are courtesy of Shutterstock and © the following
photographers: 1 & 186 STILLFX; 3 & 152 XYZ; 5 & 62 Vicente Barcelo Varona; 6bl & 178 goodboypictures; 6br & 153t TaigeR; 6t & 98
swinner; 7b & 210, 4 & 14 kentoh; 7t & 222 Vjom ; 8b & 226 Serg64; 8t & 184 Alexander Kalina; 9 & 238 Ermek; 10 & 108 Jerome
Scholler; 11 & 44 Natalia Maximova; 12 & 64, 150 Gunnar Pippel; 13 & 106 Jorge Pedro Barradas de Casais; 25 James Kingman; 27
Hywit Dimyadi; 28 marekuliasz; 41 Radu Razvan; 42 L_M_Bilder; 45 Meder Lorant; 66 Colour; 87 parfta; 111 Zsolt Nyulaszi; 120
iconspro; 123 VVO; 126 P.Uzunova; 131 Robert Spriggs; 147 Dic Liew SvetlanaIvanova; 154 Timashov Sergiy; 159b Atlaspix; 159t
keellla; 180 Tatiana Popova; 181 arfo; 183 FOTOCROMO; 188 Chad McDermott; 189 Volina; 199 Annett Goebel; 212 Santiago Cornejo

DESIGN
YOUR OWN
WEBSITE

ROGER LAING & RHYS LEWIS
CONSULTANT EDITOR: PRIYA RAVEENDRAN

FLAME TREE
PUBLISHING

CONTENTS

Before you embark on designing your own website, it is as well to understand the basic terminology. From computer basics to more complex technical terms, this section covers the fundamentals of understanding how computers and web pages work, to help you get up and running.

WEB THEORY

When planning a website, it is essential to apply some basic principles used by all good web designers. It is not enough to come up with a colour scheme that looks good on paper, for example – it may not translate well on to the screen. This chapter outlines the fundamental theories of good web design.

BASIC WEB DESIGN. 98

Now you have mastered the principles of how to set up a good website, it is time to put them into practice. This section begins with an outline of how to create a basic website, then goes into more detail about the areas of importance such as coding, image use and effects.

INTERMEDIATE WEB DESIGN. 178

Once your basic website is up and running it is time to delve a bit deeper into the web-design process. This section explains how to further develop your website, from making the most of HTML tags, through intermediate image treatments to taking advantage of search engines.

ADVANCED WEB DESIGN

This section covers the more advanced web-design techniques that will put the finishing touches to your pages, bringing them to life and really helping your viewers interact with your content and your message.

TECHNICAL MATTERS

This section explains in detail
some of the technology you will
have come across in the book,
including the different languages
used and their applications,
benefits and drawbacks, and the
server-side technology used for
dynamic content.

SOFTWARE

Using the right software is key to good web design, so here are some of the best places to start – from the best web browsers to use to the latest in image-editing software, plus the whole web-design packages to set you on your way.

INTRODUCTION

With the World Wide Web being one of the fastest-growing areas on the Internet, an increasing number of people want to take advantage of this new interactive and dynamic communications medium.

INFORMATION DESIGN

Website design has made a significant impact on the Web. It is essentially information design and is a means of communicating information to your audience. Designing websites is undeniably fun and exciting, but it is important to understand that web design is a multi-faceted field, encompassing a mixture of artistic and technological disciplines that range from graphic and user-interface design to programming and client/server technology.

Most people have some idea of what they want their website to communicate. The difficulty comes in knowing how to effectively present that idea. It is a common misconception that style is all that matters in web design, but this is not the case. What happens behind the scenes in creating a website is just as important as how it looks up front and it is essential to understand the theory and practice behind why a site works. Knowing your design and technological options means you will be conscious of their potential, regardless of whether or not you decide to use them in your pages.

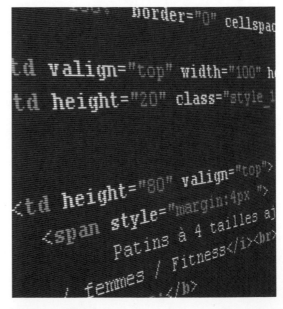

RULES OF GOOD WEB DESIGN

Good web design is hard to define, but there is an understanding of what you should and should not do. Guidelines and standards have been developed to assist web designers in creating more user-friendly pages. It is imperative to understand the motivation behind such rules rather than blindly applying them.

Websites are often developed from one particular angle or another. Some are technology-oriented (which can result in the exclusion of users who do not have the most up-to-date browsers or plug-ins), others are content-oriented (which may result in a dull, boring site) and many more are visually oriented (which can result in the overuse of graphics, leading to higher file sizes and slower page-loading times).

USABILITY

The real emphasis, however, should be on the user, without losing sight of the technological and visual factors. Usability plays an integral part in the effectiveness of a website and is directly related to user satisfaction. Meeting user needs and expectations is the key focus of user-oriented design, although it can be difficult to achieve a fine balance between designer wants and user needs. It is always important to remember that designers are not users and that users are not designers; progressive web designers need to have a solid understanding of their medium and their users.

The key to creating a successful website lies in having a sound knowledge of all the factors influencing web design and in understanding how to achieve an effective balance between them.

USING THIS BOOK

This book covers all aspects of web design and aims to give readers a wider practical and theoretical knowledge of the field. Readers are introduced to the design process and shown how to carry a website project through from concept to completion, as well as learning the basics of web terminology. The book outlines design principles for crafting effective web pages and explains the different types of graphic formats, together with their use and how to optimize them for web delivery. There is also deeper discussion of graphic techniques, explaining the use of graphic tools and various image enhancement and manipulation techniques.

Included here are the myriad software packages that are on the market. The major graphic programs such as Adobe Photoshop are covered, as well as the leading web-authoring programs. There is also information on the major web browsers and their roles in successful web design.

Readers are shown how to create web pages to professional standards, employing user interface and usability principles. The book explains the Web's technical limitations, such as bandwidth and browser compatibility, and outlines measures that can be taken to manage and overcome them.

Tutorials are offered on creating effective web pages for both personal and commercial purposes, with explanations of HTML, style sheets and the inclusion of tables and frames. The book also covers animation and shows how to add dynamic factors and interactivity to web pages.

Dozens of tips are provided, helping readers to make informed decisions and to avoid common pitfalls that some beginners experience. Also included are a number of excellent sources where readers can obtain additional information, free software, graphics and fonts.

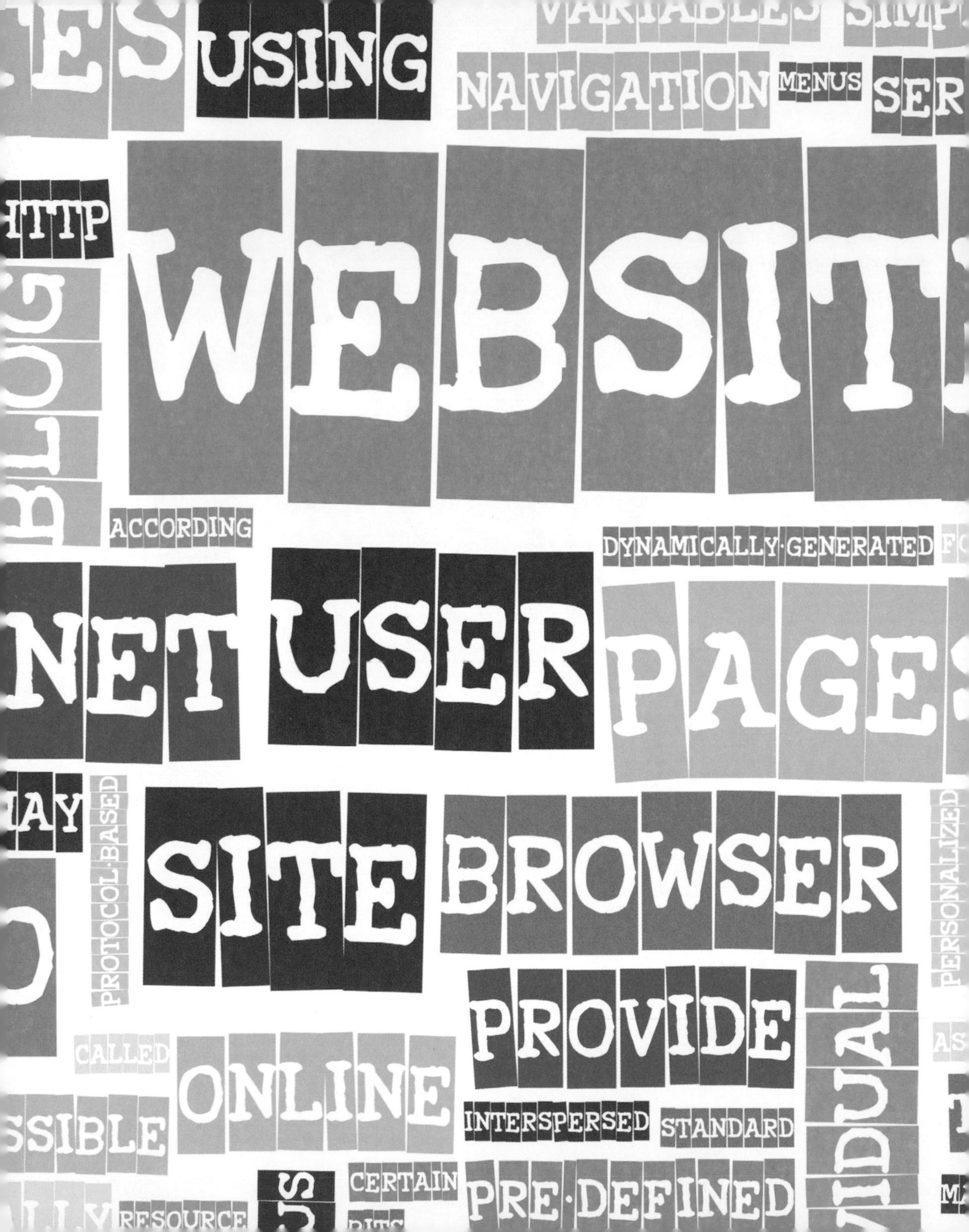

ES USING NAVIGATION MENUS SER
VARIABLES SIMP

HTTP

BLOG

WEBSIT

ACCORDING

DYNAMICALLY·GENERATED

NET USER PAGE

AY

PROTOCOL-BASED

SITE BROWSER

PERSONALIZED

PROVIDE

VIDUAL AS

CALLED ONLINE

SSIBLE INTERSPERSED STANDARD

LY US CERTAIN PRE·DEFINED VIDU M

RESOURCE ITS

WEB TERMINOLOGY

BASIC JARGON

This is terminology that even the most uninitiated computer-user will have heard of but, when it comes to web design, it is important to know exactly what these expressions mean and how they apply to your programming.

FILES

Information on the Web is stored in a variety of file types, marked by an extension. A file is a collection of information that has been given a name, or filename. There are many different kinds of files but, on the Web, the most common are data files, text files, graphics files, audio files and video files.

A basic web page is stored as a text file, although it is given the file extension of .htm or .html. Hand-coders using Notepad need to be especially careful, as this program saves documents as .txt by default. If it is not saved as .htm or .html, it will not be recognized by the browser.

Above: Saving a file as html

File Extensions

Generally, servers are sensitive to file extensions and the correct one must be used or the link to the file will not work. For instance, picture files must also have the correct suffix, such as .jpg or .jpeg for JPEGs, .gif for GIFs and .png for PNG files. It is also important to follow the naming convention supported by your web server, otherwise no file will be found.

File Types

Different file types have different file formats, or ways of organizing the information they store. These are shown by the file extension – the three or four letters that come after the period at the end of a filename. Web servers add a header to each document they send to the browser, which indicates which type of file it is. This lets the browser know how to handle the file – i.e. whether to open it in a window or launch the appropriate plug-in or helper application.

There are many file types on the Web; among the common ones are:

➔ **.htm or .html**: A web page that can be viewed by a browser or other HTML-compatible program.

➔ **.jpg**, **.glf**, **.png**: Image file formats used on the Web.

➔ **.mp3**: Because of its near CD-quality, MP3 is commonly used for distribution of music on the Web.

➔ **.rm**: Streaming video.

➔ **.avi**, **.mov**, **.mpeg**: Digital video formats.

➔ **.pdf**: Portable document format that needs the Adobe Acrobat reader (or similar application) to be viewed.

➔ **.zip**: Compressed file that needs to be unzipped (decompressed) before viewing.

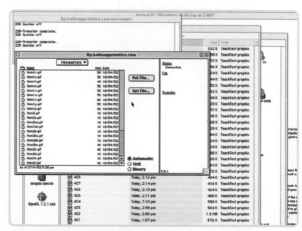

Above: Selecting image files to upload to a website

File Size

File size is critical on the Web to minimize download time, so a variety of compression techniques are used to make files smaller. The size of a file is measured by the number of bytes it takes up, where a single byte represents one letter or character. Typically, file sizes will be shown in either kilobytes (KB), which is 1,024 bytes, or megabytes (MB) which is just over a million bytes (1,048,576 bytes). Very large files may be expressed in gigabytes (GB), which is 1,000 million bytes.

Compression

To minimize file size and reduce download time, most graphics files are optimized for the Web in a compressed format. Compression works by removing repetitive information and spaces. GIF and PNG files use a 'lossless' system which does not affect the quality of the image, unlike JPEGs which use 'lossy' compression, where the file is reduced in size by removing data from the image (see page 51). HTML can also be optimized by removing excessive characters such as spacing and comments, and pages designed using cascading style sheets (CSS) are also smaller and much more efficient than HTML-only pages.

Many of the programs and files stored on the Internet are also compressed and have to be restored to their original format before being used by utilities such as WinZip (for Windows) or StuffIt Expander (for the Mac).

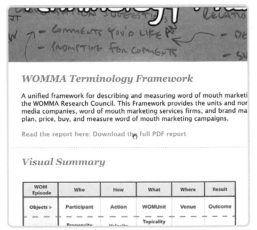

PDF

PDF is a file format that enables documents to be presented just as they originally looked, regardless of what type of computer or platform they are viewed on. Because the document keeps its original formatting, it is

Above: PDFs can be downloaded from websites via links

very popular with companies that want to put forward a consistent corporate brand across all their publications. It is also a natural for the Web, as it works cross-platform; consequently, most white papers, instruction manuals and other documents viewed or downloaded, whether on the Internet or the company intranet, are saved as PDF files (file extension .pdf).

Viewing PDFs

In order to view a PDF file in your browser, you need the special Adobe Acrobat reader, free from www.adobe.com. Within the viewer, it is possible to navigate long documents through thumbnails, enlarge the view, print the pages or even add comments. The ease of navigation and consistent formatting makes it particularly popular for e-books, especially through new security features such as digital watermarks, which help designers, writers and publishers protect their copyright.

BROWSERS

Designing a shop-window display can be difficult enough. But imagine the problems if you do not know what size window the display will be viewed through, whether the colours will show up, whether the exhibits will stay in the position they were put, or whether they can be seen at all. Yet that is the problem in designing for the Web. Not only are there slight differences in the way the browsers see each page and deal with the HTML, there are also differences between the same browsers on different platforms. The designer's challenge is to make the page as interesting as possible, making full use of the technological advances each new version of a browser brings, without alienating the audience with older browsers. The standard compromise is to assume the majority of your users will have version 7 of Internet Explorer and 2.5 of Mozilla Firefox.

Which Browser?

By far the most popular browsers are Internet Explorer and Firefox, with research showing that 58 per cent of people use Internet Explorer, 30 per cent use Firefox, and four per cent use the Mac and iPhone-based Safari and Google's new Chrome browser. The other four per cent consists of smartphone and mobile phone browsers and Internet-connected games consoles.

Above: The Mozilla Firefox browser

Above: The Internet Explorer browser

Above: The logo for Google's Chrome browser

URL

A URL (Uniform Resource Locator) gives not only the location of a site but also the protocol needed to access it. The URL of a site is its address on the World Wide Web.

http: // www.garden of stars.com

Hyper Text · World Wide Web · Domain Name · Top Level
Transfer Protocol · · · Domain

Above: The constituent parts of a URL

All websites have URLs, which not only describe the location of a page or file, but also how to access it. They are made up of two parts. The first part describes what protocol to use to access the file, such as HTTP (Hyper Text Transfer Protocol, *see* page 30) if it is for a web page, or FTP (File Transfer Program, *see* page 30) if it is for a program file. The second part gives the domain name or IP address (*see* below) where the server is located. Consequently, you could have different URLs pointing to different files at the same domain. ftp://www.companydomainname.com/program.exe would be a program downloaded using the FTP protocol, whereas http://www.companydomainname.com/index.html would load the Homepage for the site, using the HTTP protocol (*see* page30).

Domain Names

The domain name is part of the URL or address that identifies a particular website. For instance, microsoft.com is the unique name that identifies the web pages for software company Microsoft. The .com suffix reflects the type of organization the site belongs to, such as .com for commercial organizations, .gov for government and .org for non-profit bodies. This part is called the top-level domain. Other, less common domain names include .info for information services and .biz for business.

IP Addresses

In fact, domain names are really a convenience for Web users, as we find it easier to remember names rather than numbers. To locate a site on the Internet, the domain name needs to be translated into its IP address. This is a block of four numbers separated by periods. The translation of a site's domain name into the IP address needed to locate it is done by DNS servers. If one server does not know the number of a particular domain

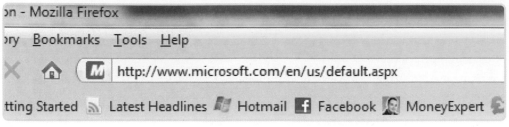

Above: URLs get longer the 'deeper' you go into a website

name, it queries another, and so on down the network, until there is a response. As you delve further down into the site, the URLs get longer and more difficult to remember. Consequently, most browsers have a facility to let you store URLs you want to visit again as Bookmarks, as they are known in Firefox, or Favorites, as they are called in Internet Explorer.

WEB HOSTING

Having completed your website, you need to find someone to host it. For personal sites and small 'brochure-style' sites, it may be sufficient to use the free web space most ISPs offer their customers. They do have drawbacks, though. Space is limited, usually the ISP's domain name is part of the URL, access speeds may be slow because many members share the same server and, with free services, there might be adverts on the site. Web hosting services also differ considerably in the special features they offer – such as free scripts and database support, all the way through to secure e-commerce facilities and streaming audio servers.

Professional Packages

Professional web-hosting packages are more flexible as they offer solutions to fit different size websites – but they come at a price. First you need to check the host uses compatible technologies (for example, UNIX-based servers will not support FrontPage extensions).

Different packages offer variable amounts of web space. If your site has hundreds of pages, or lots of graphics or audio and video files, you are going to need one of the top-end solutions.

Above: Shop around for a web hosting package that works for you

Equally, you might be better to go with a service offering unlimited data transfer rather than the typical offering of 25-50 gigabytes (GB) per month.

SERVERS

There are many different types of server which, on a local area network, are computers that manage different resources. Often, servers have a dedicated purpose; for example, a file server and linked storage devices are only used for storing files, while a print server manages traffic to and from printers. Similarly, a network server controls the administration and security of network traffic.

In a client/server architecture, such as the Internet, the server is a computer, or program, that responds to commands from a client. For example, a mail server collects and distributes messages to an email client program such as Outlook Express. On the Web, every site sits on a server, or host computer. The operating system used can be one of several types, such as UNIX, Windows or Macintosh. These all have the same function – to control communications over the Internet. In addition, there is a software program, the web server itself, which sits on the host computer and delivers the web pages requested by the client software, in this case, the browser. The web server will also carry out other browser requests, such as searching a database and returning the results together with the web page to the browser.

Server-side

In general, web programs are either client-side, meaning they are run by the browser, or server-side (*see* pages 39–41 and 236–37). Server-side programs, such as CGI scripts, run as their name suggests – on the server. They handle jobs that need access to data that is not found on the client PC. In the past, all processing was server-side, such as database-driven content where the browser handed the request to the server, which sorted it out and sent back the information with the web page.

Common Gateway Interface

Given that users operate on a range of different platforms, there needs to be a uniform way in which the browser can pass on user input and ask the server to run the correct program. This is done using the common gateway interface (CGI), a standard way of handling requests for programs. The CGI scripts themselves can be written in a number of languages, of which the most common is Perl (Practical Extraction and Report Language). There are many sites that offer scripts for anything from hit counters to online stores.

Application Programming Interface

A second way is to link the programs into the web server and database software by an API (application programming interface). This is faster, because it does not require a new program to be started at every request. However, different APIs support different servers and different programming languages.

TYPE

The type, or appearance of characters on screen, can greatly help visitors navigate through text and aids the appeal of a site. The style of type used on a computer is known as a 'typeface' or, often, a 'font' (*see below*). This is usually one of two kinds: serif, which has little strokes or curls at the end of a character; and sans-serif which does not. The most common serif typeface or font on the Web is Times, with Arial as a standard non-serif font.

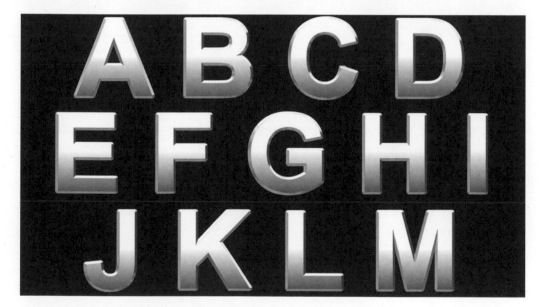

Proportional and Fixed-Width Fonts

Times and Arial are both proportional fonts, one of two basic types of font with which you will work in designing for the Web. Most text uses proportional or variable width fonts where the different letters can take up a different amount of space (e.g. 'm' spreads out while 'i' breathes in).

There are also fixed-width fonts (also called monospace), such as Courier, that give equal space to each character. They are only used with a few HTML tags such as the <pre> tag for preformatted text where each line is displayed exactly as it is written, including extra spaces, or <tt> for typewriter text.

The Full Meaning of 'Font'

The word 'font' has become synonymous with the idea of typefaces, but in fact it encompasses other features, such as the particular size, weight and spacing of the typeface. In HTML, you can specify font properties, such as size, colour or typeface, using the <font> tag, and CSS offers more control still, allowing you to alter leading (the space between lines) and word spacing.

Viewing Fonts

Even if you do specify different styles, it does not give you total control over how users will see your pages. Visitors can, in fact, override the typographical elements you set, such as the typeface or font size. You can specify a font that will override the browser default, but this will only show up if the user has that particular font on their machine.

What is more, different platforms treat font size differently. On the Macintosh, a 12-pt font appears as roughly that, while Windows, in order to make the font easier to read on screen, makes it much larger. In addition, each platform has its own range of standard fonts. So, if you specify fonts in HTML, or cascading style sheets, it is more like making a recommendation than taking firm control of what is viewed.

System Fonts

The system font is the typeface used on the Macintosh and some PC applications, in all its menus, titles and windows. It is also used to describe the base set of font combinations that come with each computer, across different platforms.

HTML editors such as Dreamweaver have preset combinations of fonts. These are made up of system fonts commonly found on most of the new computers now sold. If the user does not have the first font installed, the browser will use the second or third one specified. For example, a common combination would be <font face="Verdana, Arial, Helvetica, sans-serif">...</font>. By including a generic font family (serif, sans-serif), the browser will use one of that style if it cannot find any of the other fonts you have named.

ICONS

Icons are small pictures that are used to symbolize or represent an object or program. The most common one found on the Web is the small picture of a house used to represent the homepage. Equally, an icon of a small envelope is often put next to the mailto: link to show users they can send a message from there.

Icon Tagging

In effect, they are cute buttons, some of which will be linked to an action, some not. As they are graphical images, they are inserted on the page using the <img src="icon.gif"> tag. Use the 'alt' attribute to add some text giving an explanatory title for the icon. This way, for most users, the 'alt' text will pop up as a tip when users mouse over the image.

Using Icons

On navigation bars, icons should not be used by themselves: while it may be clear to you that the fine drawing of a spanner marks the product pages, it may not be to the user. Icons should have a title alongside, which immediately makes clear what the link is about. They should also be used sparingly; as they are pictures, they still incur some download time. Although each individual image may not be huge, if there are several on a page, the load soon adds up.

TECHNICAL JARGON

When creating your own website, you will need to get your head round some of the more technical terms you will come across. Just understanding those acronyms will not be enough – you need to know what practical applications they have.

HTML

Hypertext Markup Language – the language of the Web – is used in constructing web pages (*see also* pages 228–235 for descriptions of other web languages). In effect, it tells the browser software how to display and handle the information or objects contained on a page. It also controls the hypertext links that enable you to click from one document to another, or from one section of a page to another.

Although the HTML specifications, or recommendations, are drafted by a standards body called the World Wide Web Consortium (W3C), they have been implemented slightly differently by the major browser manufacturers, so complete cross-browser compatibility is still some way off. That said, the benefit of HTML is that it is pure text (ASCII only), so it can be read by software running on any platform.

HTML Documents

Each HTML document has two main parts: the Head, which contains general information about the file and scripts that need to be run and the Body, the content that will appear in the browser window. All HTML documents are collections of tags, enclosed within less than (<) and greater than (>) brackets. Tags can be modified by attributes which allow you to specify properties such as font, size, colour and so on.

Manual HTML Editors

To maximize their personal control over the final look of their pages, some web designers like to hand code their HTML documents. As HTML pages are plain text files, they could just use a simple text editor such as Notepad. However, if they want to speed up the process, there are HTML editors, such as HomeSite for Windows or BBEdit for the Macintosh. Unlike the 'what you see is what you get' (WYSIWYG, *see* below) authoring tools, such as Adobe's Dreamweaver or Microsoft's Expression Web, you cannot build your page visually.

With HTML editors, you need to know how to write HTML by hand, but they make the process quicker and more efficient. For instance, when they open a new document, they will automatically insert the doctype declaration and the main <head> and <body> tags. There are shortcuts for inserting different types of code – scripts as well as HTML. These are displayed in different colours to make it easier for error-checking later. The HTML editor will also let you preview the page in a number of target browsers.

WYSIWYG

There are many ways to create HTML pages but, for the beginner, the easiest is with WYSIWYG ('what you see is what you get') programs. Web-authoring tools such as Adobe Dreamweaver have become the Web equivalent of page layout tools like InDesign. As WYSIWYG HTML editors, they let you build and view the pages graphically, just as they will appear in the browser. You can draw tables, add images and set up text styles without ever looking at the HTML code or typing in a tag.

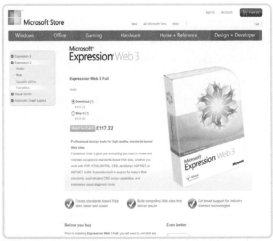

Above: Microsoft's Expression Web is a WYSIWIG web editor

HTML Pages in Practice

In practice, if you want to get beyond a fairly simple page, you do need to have a basic understanding of the code behind web design. To make it easier, Dreamweaver lets you split the page view so you have the graphical page view below and the code for it above.

One note of caution, though. While your page may look good in the preview browser of your WYSIWYG HTML editor, that is no guarantee it is going to look the same for your visitors who will be accessing your site through a variety of browsers viewed on desktops of different resolutions.

HTTP

Hypertext Transfer Protocol is the standard set of rules, or protocol, for passing files and other information (collectively known as resources) around the Web. These resources could be HTML files, image files, query results or anything else. HTTP is usually seen at the beginning of the URL, or address, for websites.

How HTTP Works

HTTP sets out how messages between the client (the browser) and the server are formatted and transmitted, and what actions they need to take following any commands they receive. For example, when you enter a URL in your browser's address bar, this sends an HTTP command to a web server, telling it to get and send back the web page you asked for. After sending its response, the server shuts down its connection, so HTTP is known as a stateless protocol. That is, it does not maintain any connection between transactions. Because it has no record of what has happened before, it is difficult to set up websites that react to a flow of user input, but this is compensated for by newer technologies using ActiveX, Java, JavaScript and cookies.

FTP

File Transfer Protocol is the fastest, most efficient way to transfer files, particularly over the Internet. On the Internet, there is a separate protocol, the Hypertext Transfer Protocol (HTTP, *see above*) used by browsers for transferring ordinary web pages and any small graphics files used. However, for the vast stocks of software, music files and archives available on the Internet, something more structured is needed. FTP covers the type or error checking in force during transmission, the compression used and how the computers will mark that they have finished sending or receiving data. Using FTP, a client program, such as CuteFTP (www.cuteftp.com) or Fetch for the Mac (http://fetchsoftworks.com/), connects to the server that holds the files wanted.

FTP sites usually offer a much wider selection of files than ordinary sites are able to. To store as many as possible, most files will be compressed. Downloads from FTP servers are also quicker than from a web server. As the fastest and most efficient way of moving files between computers, FTP is also used to upload completed web pages from your computer to a web server.

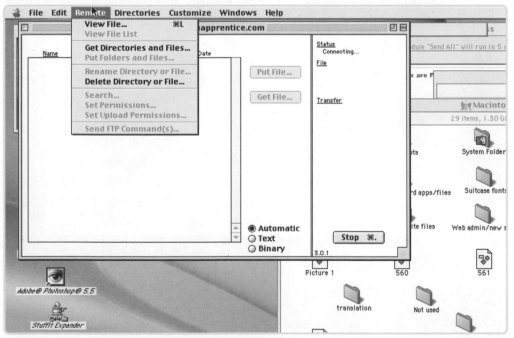

Above: Selecting files to upload to an FTP site

SPLASH PAGES

In the early days of the Internet, most sites had a splash page that was the entry point to the site. Rather like the name plate on a door, with a welcome mat underneath, it did little more than let you know you were in the right place. Then came Flash, which lived up to its name and brought some glitter to the Web, but at a cost in bandwidth and annoyance to users. Flash proved to be a distraction rather than something fundamental to the appeal of the site. This is changing, however, and rather than just being a chance for designers to show off, it is often used to create memorable effects and to reinforce brands.

Above: The splash page for the Welsh Rugby Union

Using a Splash Page

Even so, there are a number of factors to consider before deploying a splash page, particularly the purpose it is intended to serve. Does it, for example, give the user a choice between watching the Flash movie unfold or clicking straight through to the site itself? Does it offer different viewing options, or is it a required disclaimer for financial services sites or sites where there are minimum age requirements?

In terms of the content, the splash page should have full details of the site with contact links and an idea of its purpose. Most importantly, so as not to frustrate repeat visitors, it should offer a 'skip intro' link so that the intro animation does not have to be viewed each time visitors return.

POP-UPS

A pop-up is a Graphical User Interface display area, usually a small window, that suddenly appears up in the foreground of the visual interface. A pop-up window should be smaller than the background window or interface, otherwise it is a replacement interface.

While it is good to have links on your page, if people follow them – particularly to external sites – they might not come back. One solution to this problem is to open a linked page in a new browser window that will pop-up (hence its name) on screen while your existing page remains underneath. Pop-ups are also useful for presenting extra information (such as terms and conditions or product descriptions) that may not need an entire new page.

Creating Pop-ups

There are two ways to create a pop-up window: one uses HTML but has the drawback that you cannot control the size of the window; the other, more flexible but also more complicated, is to use JavaScript. (Strictly speaking, pop-up windows created by HTML are not pop-ups at all, but targets. True pop-ups are the ones controlled by JavaScript.)

In HTML, the way to create a pop-up window is to add the 'target' attribute to the anchor tag. This opens a separate window to the one displaying the current document. You cannot alter the dimensions of the new window, but it is usually a similar size to the one already open.

If you set the target to "_blank", clicking on the link will open a new window. If you use this on several links, you could soon have enough windows to set up a double-glazing factory. The solution is to give the target window a name – such as "gallery" – which can be used as a target for each link. This way, each link will open in the same "gallery" window (e.g. <a href="http://www.msn.com" target="gallery">...</a>).

JavaScript Pop-ups

To go one step further and control the size of the pop-up window and other features, you need to use JavaScript. The script itself goes in the <head> of the document. It is enclosed in comment tags <– ... //–> so older browsers that do not support JavaScript will ignore it.

In the <body> of the page, before the URL of the link, there is a reference to the fact it is JavaScript and the function that is involved – here, that is the window.open( ) method.

Setting Values

Within the script itself, you can specify the height and width of the window in pixels. By setting the values to either yes or no, you can also switch on or off other features, such as whether the new window has a toolbar, status bar or scrollbars, and whether the user can resize it. Several web-authoring tools will automatically generate the code for pop-up windows for you. Alternatively, there are several free scripts available online that can be copied and, with a little customization, used on your own pages.

SITE MAPS

Site maps are an overview of the site structure, designed to help users find their way around your website. Not only does a site map provide an overall view of your site's structure, it should

Above: There are sites available which can automatically create a site map for your website

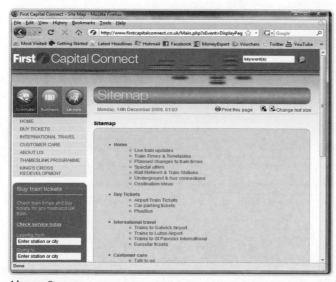

Above: Site map

also have direct links to each of the main content sections.

The common analogy to a site map is a table of contents in a book. Without having to leaf through all the pages in the book, a table of contents shows the chapter headings and the main information they contain. Similarly, the site map does not list all the pages, but it gives a hierarchical view of the main sections and content.

Setting Up a Site Map

To save on download time, it is usually easier to use a text-based site map rather than a graphical one. Setting it within a table makes it easier to format. Small sites probably do not need a site map, but for larger sites it not only helps navigation, but it can also aid search engine placement, as it makes it easier for the search engine spider to discover all the site's pages.

SCRIPTS

The distinction between programs and scripts is increasingly blurred. They both issue commands to tell the server (or browser) what to do. However, traditional programs are written in a heavyweight programming language such as C++, Java or Visual Basic, while scripts are written in the more specialized scripting languages such as Perl or JavaScript. The scripts are run line by line through a script 'interpreter', which actions the commands. By contrast, programs, which tend to be more complex, have to be compiled into machine code which can be handled directly by the computer's processor. Scripting languages also tend to be more focused on the area in which they are used. So, for example, with JavaScript, which is purely designed for use on the Web, instructions centre on refining what the browser does, checking for plug-ins, browser versions, etc.

Using Scripts

As they are usually designed for a specific task, scripting languages are fairly easy to understand, even for complete novices. There are also many ready-made scripts freely available to download from the Web at sites like www.scriptsearch.com. These cover both client-side scripting, such as JavaScript and Server-side scripts like Perl and CGI.

PHP

The 'PHP: Hypertext Preprocessor' (PHP) allows web developers to create dynamic content that interacts with databases. PHP applications work in conjunction with MySQL databases. If you intend to install software such as interactive forums, blogging tools or a CMS like Joomla to your web server, you will probably be using PHP. Check with your hosting company that your package supports PHP – Windows-based packages will support ASP instead. Originally standing for 'Personal Home Page', PHP is now one of the many computer-related examples of a recursive acronym.

BYTE

A byte is a basic unit of storage, used as a measure of file size and, more generally, a computer's capacity. The term 'byte' comes from the phrase 'binary term'. A byte is the smallest unit of storage on a computer that can hold a single character, such as a number, letter or symbol. Under the binary system, it is made up from eight bits where each bit can have one of just two values: 0 or 1.

Bit Depth

In graphics files, the number of colours is shown by its bit depth – that is, the number of bits used to represent each pixel of information in a file. For example, a one-bit image is monochrome; an 8-bit image supports 256 colours or shades of grey; and a 24-bit image includes 16.7 million colours. However, in design for print media, few systems have been able to cope with or print at more than 8-bit. The higher the bit depth, the larger the file size.

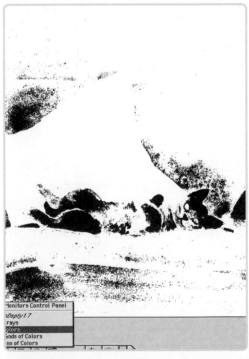

Above: A 1–bit bitmap image

Above: An 8–bit greyscale image

Above and right: A 16–bit RGB image and a 24–bit CMYK image. They look identical in print, as an image has to be converted to CMYK for print publishing.

The file size itself is measured in bytes. For example, a Word file that took up one megabyte (1MB) of space would be able to store just over a million individual characters, roughly equivalent to 2,100 pages of information. More generally, a computer's capacity, such as its memory and disk space, is measured in bytes.

PLUG-INS

Plug-ins take the idea of helper applications one stage further. Whereas a helper application is an external program, like the compression tool WinZip, that runs outside of the browser, plug-ins are better integrated. They run within the browser and extend the browser's capabilities, such as the Flash plug-in that runs the Flash-created animations used on some web pages.

Similarly, the Adobe Acrobat plug-in lets you view PDF files in your browser, rather than having to download the files and launch a separate program to read them.

Downside to Plug-ins

There are drawbacks with plug-ins. Users have to locate the plug-ins they need and install them, sometimes having to restart the computer before they operate. To compensate, later versions are self-installing and browsers now come with a set of plug-ins as standard. Most are geared towards multimedia players, such as Flash and Shockwave, QuickTime, RealVideo and RealAudio. Even so, updates are constantly emerging and it may be that, although you have the plug-in, you still need to download a newer version to play the file. Design-wise, plug-ins can easily be included on the web page using the <embed> tag, or the more favoured <object> tag.

CLIENTS

Clients can either be the PCs themselves or the programs on them that rely on servers to carry out certain services for them. Typically, a client PC is linked, either through a physical network or, in the case of the Internet, over phone lines, to a server. The 'back-end' server – also called the host computer – carries out certain services for the 'front-end' client program, which runs on the PC. For example, a mail server delivers or sends messages that have been written in a client program, such as Outlook.

Another client program is your browser. Type in a URL in the address bar of the browser and the request goes first to a DNS (Domain Name System) server that translates that address into a network location. It then goes to the web server, which processes the request and returns the page.

Client-side Programs

Client-side scripts are written directly within the HTML code, embedded between the <script> and </script> tags in the head of the document. Putting them here ensures that the scripts are read before the rest of the HTML page. The scripts carry out the actions requested. So, for

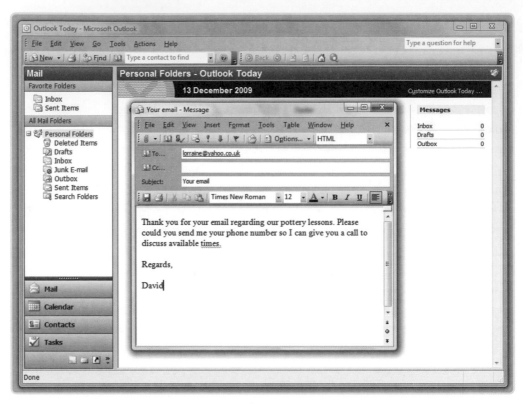

Above: Mail programs, such as Outlook Express, are client–side programs

example, in rollovers, the script enables the colour of the background to change when a mouse moves across it. Client-side scripts can also swap one image for another, validate form data before it is sent to the server, or 'sniff' for which type of browser is accessing the site and show different content accordingly.

Most scripts are written in JavaScript, although Microsoft browsers also support VBScript (*see* page 234). Some Java applets also work client-side. JavaScript support is variable in browsers and can be turned off altogether by users, so it is a good idea to embed alternative content between the <noscript>...</noscript> tags for browsers that do not understand scripting.

Server-side Programs

Web servers (*see* pages 24 and 236–37) can also run a number of other server-side scripts and programs, such as querying a database, and return the results, together with the HTML page, for viewing through a browser. Clients are part of a client/server architecture that runs applications by combining the performance of standalone PCs with the data management, information sharing, security features and processing power of servers.

BANDWIDTH

Designing for the Web was once limited by the amount of bandwidth available to the average user and, before the advent of widespread broadband access, bandwidth was the great constraining factor on web design. Technically, bandwidth is a measure of the amount of data that can be transmitted in a fixed amount of time. It is usually shown as bits per second (bps) or more frequently in thousands of bits per second (Mbps). The greater the bandwidth, the faster data can be sent.

Broadband

Even though most of us now view sites over broadband links, high-speed access is no reason to ignore one of the fundamentals of site design. Superfluous images are only likely to annoy users who have to wait for them to download, and high-resolution graphics and large Flash files are still better off avoided if there is a danger that their addition will merely slow down the arrival of other, more important elements on your page, such as text or navigation tools. Video is another bandwidth hog: if you are adding clips to your site, make sure the resolution is not so high that your visitors will be left frustrated by a video that stops every three or four seconds as it loads.

VIEWING JARGON

How your website looks is key to its success. But exactly how does the technology work to create the visuals your visitor sees? Here is the terminology behind those all-important visuals.

PIXELS

A pixel is the smallest element on screen that can be individually controlled. These pixels are arranged on a grid over the screen; each pixel (short for picture elements) on screen is made up of a set of three individual dots (red, green and blue) which are combined to create a particular colour. Although the dots are separate, they are close enough to appear as a single blended colour – or virtual pixel – to the human eye.

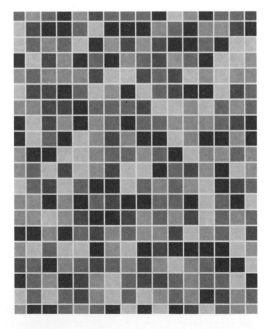

Colour and Brightness

When you open an image, web page or program, the computer changes the colour and brightness of each pixel to reproduce the image or text. The number of colours shown depends on the number of bits used to send information to each pixel. With a 1-bit monitor, it is quite simple, the pixel is either off or on. When the colour depth (also known as pixel depth) is 8-bits, greater variety is possible. The pixel can handle 8 bits of information at once which gives 256 possible combinations. 24-bit monitors or images can display up to 16.7 million colours (*see also* pages 36–37).

SCREEN RESOLUTION

The screen resolution is the total number of pixels available. This will depend not only on the physical size of the monitor (15-in, 19-in, etc.), but also on the capabilities of the video card driving it. For instance, on a 17-in monitor, you could have several settings ranging from 800 x 600 (800 dots, or pixels, on each of 600 lines) to 1280 x 1024. As you increase the number of pixels, the pixels will get smaller as you are packing more into the same available space. This means that your images and other on-screen elements will appear smaller. As a result, more can be seen on the screen.

Checking Resolution

To cope with the different screen resolutions, web browsers effectively ignore it. In a browser, one image pixel equals one screen pixel. If your graphic is 300 pixels wide and 200 pixels tall, it is displayed on exactly the same number of pixels on screen. So, if the screen resolution is set higher, that number of pixels will take up a smaller area and the picture will appear smaller. The converse is true if the resolution is set lower.

Consequently, in designing elements of your web page, you will not know exactly how big or small they will be viewed by your visitors, but you will see how they measure up in proportion to each other.

WEB-SAFE COLOURS

Web-safe colours provide a consistent view from low spec machines to the highest, but impose other limitations. The web palette is a selection of 216 colours that will not dither (*see* page 44) on PCs or Macs. It is built into all the main system and browser palettes.

Why Choose from the Web Palette?

If you designed a GIF with non web-safe colours, it would appear with some shifting and dithering on an 8-bit monitor. That is because the browser compensates for the lack of colours the monitor can display by blending (dithering) other colours together to approximate the

ones it needs. By using web-safe colours in the graphics you design, you can be sure they will look as good on 8-bit monitors as any others. As most images will display properly on 16- and 24-bit monitors, it is really only an issue for 8-bit resolution monitors (that can only display 256 colours). It also does not affect photographic images or JPEG files in the same way.

The benefit of using the web palette (also referred to as Web216, browser-safe and non-dithering) in your designs is that they will have a consistent look for all users across platforms. However, the colour selection is not the greatest and does have its limitations. (*See also* page 80.)

DITHERING

The number of colours a monitor can display depends on its bit depth. A 24-bit monitor can show millions of colours, while an 8-bit colour monitor can only display 256. Although a 24-bit colour monitor is not going to have any problems displaying an image with thousands of colours, the 8-bit monitor does. The browser's workaround is to dither the extra colours, i.e. it blends two of the colours it does have in its palette to approximate the additional ones it needs. The result can make the images look rather speckled and there is the added complication that browsers on different systems have different palettes to which they refer to mix their colours.

One way to solve this problem – at least for the flat-colour GIF files that are mainly affected by it – is to only use colours in the web-safe palette (*see* above and pages 79–81). Consequently, the colours will appear the same, or as near as they are ever likely to, whichever computer they are viewed on.

USABILITY

A guaranteed way to drive visitors away from your site is to create an unfriendly, slow-loading interface. But usability does not have to mean bland, image-free pages, it is just a case of understanding how users will find their way around the site.

Page Structure

Do not waste everyone's time on splash pages and unnecessary animated graphics. Splash screens say very little that placing your company logo in a prominent position cannot, and anything that delays a user's entry to the site could well turn them away for good. Site-wide consistency is vital. The basic page structure should be the same, and the navigation menu should be in the same place on every page, with 'alt' attributes for each menu button.

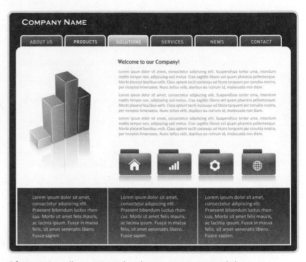

Above: A well-structured website increases usability

Sticking to Web Conventions

Web conventions must be adhered to. Do not underline text, especially in blue, as users will mistake it for a hyperlink, and, conversely, make the links stand out to the reader. Try to avoid making a page too wide, as few users enjoy having to scroll horizontally. When preparing a site, watch as colleagues have a look around the pages and gauge how easily they navigate through. When the site is live, get more user feedback to increase usability and attract more visitors.

Metaphors

Whether using an image-based metaphor, or traditional text-based links, it is important that the user interface is consistent and clear. To help understand the mass of information available on site, some designers use a metaphor to represent the way the web pages are structured. Instead of a largely text-based home page, the interface is shown as a town or a room, such as a doctor's surgery. Then each section is represented by some object – such as pills for medicines, a scalpel or other instruments for surgery, books for reference, etc.

Such imagery does have drawbacks: it is graphics heavy, which can slow download time and not everything may fit the metaphor neatly, particularly as a site expands. However, limited use, such as with particular tools, can work well. The classic example is the shopping cart. Everyone knows it from the real world and the same metaphor fits the virtual store.

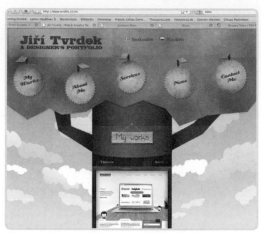

Above: This website uses a tree bearing fruit as a metaphor to help ease and enliven navigation

Consistency

Consistency and clarity also help make a user interface user friendly. For instance, navigational tools should be placed consistently through the site, not moved around. Sections should be called the same throughout and labels should make it clear what they are about. Links should look like links. Text links should be coloured the same throughout the site. Traditionally, this has been blue and underlined. However, using HTML and cascading style sheets, it is possible to have different styles for links, mouse-overs and visited links, etc. Whatever you choose, it should be the same throughout the site and it should stand out from the rest of the text.

Eye Flow

Web pages can be so busy that a first-time visitor may find it hard to work out where to start. By laying out pages according to certain rules, you can guide readers around the screen and offer a comfortable and engaging browsing experience. The reader's eye naturally flows from left to right and from top to bottom. The smoother that process is, the more information will be received and processed.

When a page is opened, the reader's eye will fall on the top left-hand corner of the page. This may be where the site banner or menu is placed, and is probably not an ideal starting point. To emphasize where you want your reader to begin, contrast it significantly from the other elements at the top of the page – use a contrasting colour or bold font so that it stands out, or a large, bright logo which pulls the eye in. Crosses work particularly well in this respect.

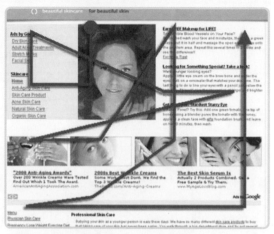

Above: A badly–designed web page directs the user's eye flow in a haphazard manner

Make sure all your pages are top-heavy. Once the reader is hooked in, guide them gently down the page by reducing the emphasis, breaking up paragraphs with light subheads. The least important page elements can go where the eye is least likely to notice, in the far right-hand side. Play them down using smaller text and subtle graphics.

INTERACTIVITY

Interactivity on the Web enables users to customize what they see, what they do and even what they buy. When a web page is posted on the Internet, it is said to be published. But what separates the Web from most other types of publication is the degree of interaction there is. This exchange is not only between the site and the users, but also between users themselves, particularly with online games and chat.

At the most basic level, interaction comes simply by clicking on a link that takes you from one page to another. Equally, that link can move you from one site to another halfway across the world.

Above: Interactivity exists in the form of online games

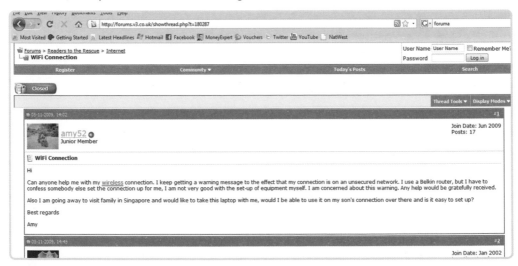

Above: The interactivity of forums enables users to share problems and advice

Scripting

Client-side scripting, such as JavaScript, and DHTML (*see* below and page 229), will change what is on view in response to a mouse click or the position of the cursor. Click on a mailto: link and it launches your email client for instant feedback. More fundamentally, a front-end form can gather all sorts of information from the user that can then be used for many kinds of interaction. It can be posted to a database, alter the information the user sees next, or lead to the purchase of some item as part of an online store.

DYNAMIC WEB PAGES

Originally, web pages were static – the content did not change from the time the page was initially created. But now a variety of technologies have brought movement and change to the Web. Animation, whether a simple animated GIF or a flash movie, can create dynamic effects on the page. Similarly, Dynamic HTML (DHTML – *see* page 229), which is a composite of cascading style sheets (CSS), CSS positioning and JavaScript, will change what is displayed in the browser window. The movement comes either as a result of some interaction by the user or from following some script. So, for example, menus can slide out automatically, animated objects float round the window, etc.

Server-side Pages

The most dynamic sites are where content is generated by server-side programming – at the time the user asks for the page. Usually, the information is stored in a database. When the page is requested, the content is merged into page

Above: Websites that sell products, such as Amazon, use dynamic web pages

templates and delivered to the user. Dynamic web pages like this will normally be marked .asp (for Active Server Pages) or .jsp (for JavaServer pages). A typical example is a search engine page where each query results in a new page being created with the results of the search.

GRAPHICS JARGON

Images are key to a dramatic and successful website. It is therefore essential to understand which file formats are best for which types of imagery, and how to make sure the pictures you use are sending the right message.

IMAGE TYPES

Images on a computer are of two types: vector graphics and bitmap images. Vector art is created by drawing programs, such as Adobe Illustrator, and uses mathematical definitions to describe shapes and lines. Consequently, the image can be rescaled or viewed at any screen resolution and not lose any of its clarity. However, to be viewed online, most vector images need to be converted to a bitmap file format and saved as a GIF or JPEG.

Bitmaps

With bitmap images, also known as raster images, the graphic is made up of rows and columns of dots. Each dot of the image is mapped on screen to individual pixels. In addition, each pixel has a colour value, which is determined by the bit depth. With black and white images, one bit equals one dot, but for colours each dot is represented by several bits of data.

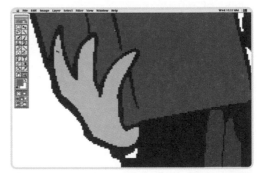

Consequently, bitmaps are good at showing subtle shades and colours and so are used for continuous-tone images such as photographs. However, as bitmaps are represented by a fixed number of pixels, they do not scale well and will appear jagged and fuzzy.

Above: Rasterized images can only be used reliably at up to 100% of their size, otherwise they may pixellate (appearing jagged or fuzzy)

JPEG

The best file format for images with lots of subtle colours, JPEG compression does involve a trade-off between image quality and file size. JPEG is the best format to use for images such as photographs, which have lots of subtle colours blended together. It is also good with greyscale images. The format is named after the Joint Photographic Experts Group, the standards body that developed it. The file extension is .jpg or .jpeg.

Compression Techniques

Because they support 24-bit colour, JPEGs can contain millions of colours, compared to the GIF, which is restricted to a palette of 256 colours. JPEGs are widely used on the Web because the compression algorithm they use can reduce file sizes significantly and shorten download time. The technique involved is called 'lossy compression', whereby redundant information is removed. As a result, when an image is heavily compressed, quite a lot of the detail is lost and blotchy squares of colours, referred to as artifacts, may appear.

The lossy compression technique also means that, once image quality is reduced, it cannot be replaced. So, if you resave a JPEG as another JPEG you lose even more image quality. For that reason, it is better to keep the original version intact and, when you want to change something, go back to that and save it as a JPEG.

Image Quality

With JPEGs, the more you compress the file, the worse the image looks. However, it is better at compressing smooth, even blurred images than those with sharp edges. You can use this to your advantage when optimizing graphics by opening the image in your picture editor and softening it. You do this by applying the Gaussian Blur filter or, in Fireworks, the

Above: Using Gaussian blur to soften an image before compressing

Smoothing tool. As always, you need to be careful that you do not trade too much image quality for better compression and a smaller file size.

Progressive JPEGs

JPEGs can also be downloaded in sections, in the same way as interlaced GIFs (see below). In progressive JPEGs, a blurred, very low resolution version of the image is downloaded that gradually becomes clearer and more detailed. With some graphics programs, you can set how many passes it takes to complete the image. For viewers, it has the advantage that they see a rough version of the graphic before it fully downloads. Unfortunately, some of the earlier browsers do not support progressive JPEGs.

GIF

The Graphics Interchange Format was the first and is still one of the most popular formats for online graphics. Pronounced with a hard G, the GIF was initially created by the online service pioneer CompuServe. Its popularity stems from the fact that it is cross-platform, so can be viewed on any computer, and that it compresses files to save download time. It uses a 'lossless' system, whereby there is no degradation in the quality of the image. However, it may mean that the file size is larger than a similar image as a JPEG, which uses a 'lossy compression' scheme in which nonessential or repetitive data is removed from the image to make the file smaller.

As a result, GIFs are best used for images with a few flat blocks of colour, such as logos or simple illustrations. Where there are subtle changes in colour, it is better to use JPEGs, which can support 24-bit colour. GIFs are 8-bit and can only have 256 colours. Graphics packages such as Fireworks or Photoshop also let you apply transparency to areas of a GIF so that its background blends in with the background colour or image on your site, and for animation.

GIF89a

The main advantage of this newer GIF standard is its support for transparency. This allows you to make one of the colours invisible – often the bottom one – in order for the background colour of the web page to show through. Without it, there would be an ugly white box around many of the graphics on the Web.

GIF89a (named rather inelegantly after the year it was developed) also supports interlacing. This is where graphics flow on to the page either row by row or column by column and means that a rough version of the graphic appears before the whole image is downloaded.

Animated GIF

This graphics file format is a simple but effective way to bring some action to your web pages. Animated GIFs work in much the same way as flipping through a cartoon book: several images are combined into a single GIF file and the animation effect is produced by rotating through them in sequence.

The compact GIF file can be put on your web page like any other graphics file. The original images can be composed in your regular graphics program. It is advisable to restrict the number of images – or frames – you use, as the more there are, the bigger the file size and the longer the download time. The individual frames are put together in sequence in a graphics program such as Adobe Fireworks or a utility specially created for building animated GIFs. Here, you set such features as the delay between frames and the number of times you want the animation to repeat (loop).

While animated GIFs are not as smooth or clever as animations produced in other formats, they are extremely popular because of their low file-size and the fact they can be viewed in nearly all browsers without the need for any additional viewer or plug-in.

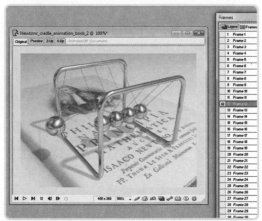

Above: This GIF consists of a number of frames that combine to create an animation

PNG

In many ways, the PNG (Portable Network Graphics, pronounced 'ping') format combines most of the best features of its rivals GIF and JPEG. It was specially designed as an open standard for Web graphics back in the mid-1990s but, despite its many attractive features, the format has been slow to take off, largely because it is not widely supported by browsers. That said, most of the well-known graphics programs do allow you to save files in the PNG format.

Although, like JPEGs, PNG can support millions of colours, it uses a lossless compression technique. Consequently, it will invariably create bigger files than JPEG's lossy compression when used on the same image.

Benefits of PNGs

PNGs are more usually seen as a substitute for GIFs. The compression is better, resulting in smaller file sizes. They support interlacing, and images will appear up to eight times faster than with traditional GIFs. This is because they fill in information in two dimensions (both rows and columns) as opposed to one with GIFs. They also allow for transparent backgrounds and it is even possible to vary the level of transparency for special transition effects.

Above: Saving an image as a PNG file

TIFF

The TIFF (Tag Image File Format) is widely used for saving scanned images before being converted into other file types more convenient for the Web. TIFF is one of the most widely used file formats for bitmapped images, particularly in the print world, as it is cross-platform and supported on many operating systems, including Windows, UNIX and the Macintosh. Files in the TIFF format have .tif as the extension.

It was originally developed by scanner manufacturers looking for a standard file format for desktop publishing. Consequently, it is very colour accurate and many designers prefer to save scanned images as TIFF files, before converting them into other formats such as GIF, JPEG or PNG for the Web.

TIFF Compression

The TIFF format compresses files using the same lossless compression technique adopted in GIF files. The LZW compression method looks for pixels or image elements of the same colour that can be described as a unit.

Above: Using the LZW compression method

IMAGE RESOLUTION

Image resolution is a measure of how sharp and clear an image is. Normally, it is measured in terms of pixels per inch (ppi) or, for printed images, in dots per inch (dpi), although often the two terms are used interchangeably.

Ideal Resolution

The ideal resolution for an image often depends on where it will be displayed. If the image is going to be printed out, it would typically be around 300 dpi. On the Web, there is no need for it to be such high resolution. All images should be low resolution, as they will ultimately be viewed on low-res screens.

Traditionally, the highest resolution on a monitor was in the region of 72 dpi and, although newer monitors have a wider range, it is still standard practice to create images at 72 dpi. In fact, it is not so much the number of pixels per inch that is important, but the number of pixels in total. On the Web, graphics map one-on-one with the screen pixels so, no matter what the resolution, a 600 pixel-wide banner will fit 600 pixels. On a high-resolution monitor, this will appear smaller than on a lower-resolution monitor.

IMAGE MANIPULATION

With the power of web-graphics editors, a basic image does not need to stay basic for long. It can be significantly improved by a relatively simple addition, such as a coloured border. While most graphics packages have a range of borders that can be used, they need to be applied to a flattened image. If your graphic has more than one layer, it needs to be flattened before the border is applied.

Improving Images

There are a number of tools that enable you to gloss over any faults on the image. Using the Clone brush, you can copy (clone) from one part of an image to another to cover any flaw in the background. A Retouch tool enables you to apply special effects to a section of an image rather than to the entire graphic. It is useful if you want to lighten colours or emboss a part of the image. More fundamentally, you can alter the orientation of an image by flipping it (reversing an image along its vertical axis) or mirroring it; that is, reversing it horizontally so what was on the left side becomes the right and what was on the right appears on the left.

Colour Channels

Colour information about images is stored in channels. These channels can be split in different ways, such as HSL (Hue, Saturation and Light) or RGB (Red, Green and Blue) and CMYK (Cyan, Magenta, Yellow and blacK). Filters or masks can be applied to the individual channels to create interesting effects, and the channels recombined. When you split an image into its channels, it creates new images, so the original is unaffected by any changes.

Altering Colour

To create the brown sepia effect of old photographs, you use a colourize command, which provides a uniform level of hue and saturation while leaving the lightness values unchanged. Alternatively, the posterize effect gives an image a flatter look with bands of colour rather than a smooth gradient, achieved by reducing the number of bits per colour channel. It is also possible to generate a 'negative image' using the function that replaces each pixel colour with its opposite on the colour wheel. So, if the brightness value of the pixel is 30, its negative is 225.

Above: Using the 'watercolour' effect filter

Distortion

Most graphics programs also come with a set of special effects that can be applied to distort your picture, give it a textured look, or appear in 3D. Similarly, you can blur or soften an image by applying filters that smooth the transitions and alter the contrast around the edges by averaging the pixel colours. Alternatively, you can apply different filters to enhance the edges of an image by increasing the contrast.

CACHING IMAGES

In the battle to minimize download time, the browser cache is very useful. When any graphics are downloaded, they are automatically stored in the cache, saved to the web visitor's hard drive or memory so that, if they are needed again, they can be displayed pretty much instantly. As a result, if you use the same graphic – such as an icon or part of a navigation bar – several times, it costs nothing in download time after the first use.

Image Store

The cache can also be used to download large image files and store them until they need to be displayed. Preloading images is done quite simply, by putting the graphic on an early page (such as the homepage) that is likely to be accessed and read first. But the trick is to set the 'width' and 'height' attributes to one pixel, such as <img src="largepic.gif" width="1" height="1">. This way, the image will only appear as a one-dot pixel (which can be placed somewhere unobtrusive) but will download with the rest of the page. When the user then goes to the page where the image is positioned full size, it will be loaded instantly from the cache.

WATERMARK

Traditionally, a watermark has been used on special printed paper to authenticate its origins and attest to its quality. It is most noticeably seen with currency, where watermarks are added to help prevent counterfeiting. In the same way, designers, writers and publishers are looking to protect the copyright in their creations using digital watermarks. The watermark can hold all sorts of information, such as who owns the copyright, the audience for which it is intended, and whether it is royalty free or restricted in its use. The watermarks are only visible in software that can read it – currently possible with Digimarc, the PictureMarc plug-in for Adobe Photoshop and for Adobe Acrobat PDF files.

Above: Digital watermarks protect images from abuse of copyright

A background image can also be used as a watermark on a web page. This differs from usual backgrounds in that the watermark does not move when you scroll the page. It means taking some care in the design of your page to make sure the watermark does not obscure any content that scrolls over it. It is also a feature that does not have universal browser support.

IMAGE LICENSING

Photo libraries license use of their images in different ways. Most have very specific, individual agreements which you should read carefully before purchasing any artwork. Generally, though, pictures are licensed for one-time use on a specific project or are offered as part of a royalty-free collection and can be used many times on many projects.

Royalty-free Images

An example of the royalty-free method is Clipart.com (http://www.clipart.com/), which works on a subscription basis. Once you pay your weekly or monthly fee, you can download and use as many photos, illustrations, buttons or fonts as you want. Like all royalty-free graphics, there are still restrictions, such as the images not being used for 'obscene' or 'scandalous' works.

Rights-managed Images

More traditional photo libraries sell a licence to use their images. The price will vary depending on where

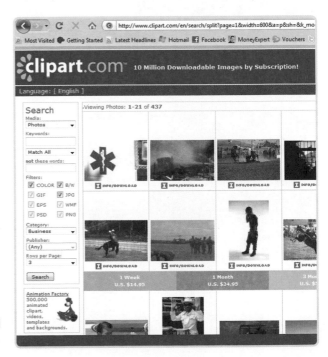

Above: Clipart.com is one of many royalty–free image libraries

and when the image will be used, how big it will be reproduced and what its intended purpose is. Note that some image libraries, such as Corbis (www.corbis.com) charge a lower fee if the picture is for editorial use (in a magazine or on a website) rather than being used commercially for advertising or promotional purposes.

Above: Corbis is one of many rights-managed image libraries. They also sell royalty-free images.

```
                                    else {
t(fcomplex z)}                      ans=x*sqrt(1
fcomplex c;                         temp=x/y;
float w;                            ans=y*sqr
if(mp(z/-r == 0.0)                 }
} ans=y*sq   c.r=0.0;       return ans;
} else {     c.i=0.0;
             w = sqrt((sqrt(z.-
             if (z.r )= 0.0)(
                            c.r=w;
        } else {            c.i=z.i/(2.
f(omplex:Csqrt(fcompl
urn fc;           }
urn(fc;omplex{z)
                         fcomplex c;
ex)RCmul(float x, f(omfloat w;
   fcomplex c;             if ((z.r == 0.0) &
   c.r=x*a.r;(z.i = 0.0)
   c.i=x*a.i;                        c.r=0.0;
   return c;
   c.i=0.0;                          c.i=0.0;
ex { Cinv( fcomplex z} else {
ex c;    sqrt((sqrt(z.rtz}     w = sqrt
```

WEB THEORY

BASIC PRINCIPLES

It is essential to understand a few basic principles before you start on your web design – not just about how the pages should look, but also the implications of choosing certain styles and formats.

TOP TIPS

Designers learning Internet skills should remember these pointers to good web design.

➔ **Don't reinvent the wheel:** Have a good browse around the Web and, when you find a site layout you like, view its source code to see how it is constructed. Many web-editing packages include a set of standard templates and themes, one of which should meet your needs.

➔ **Finalize design and templates:** Get your site design finalized and create templates before you start laying out pages. This will guarantee consistency and save you from having to re-edit every page just to correct a small problem. Likewise, plan your site structure using a flow chart.

➔ **Be strict with colours:** Select a scheme of complementary colours before you begin and do not stray from these colours. Even changing colours slightly for different site sections is inadvisable, as readers might think they have been sent to an external site.

Choose a consistent screen resolution and colour depth: Consider working with the reasonable lowest common denominator of 800 x 600-pixel screens and a 216-colour web-safe palette: a high-resolution screen and dithered colours could render your site unreadable on low-specification machines.

Keep file sizes small: Larger graphics and lengthy pages with Flash files and videos take longer to load and could prompt users to press the dreaded Back button. Compress image files as much as possible and include text alternatives in each image tag.

Avoid scrolling: Reports state that readers are reluctant to scroll down for more than one and a half screens, so it is better to run a longer story on to a second page than to force users to scroll away from the page header and navigation bar.

Do not use too many images: Graphics-heavy pages take longer to download and a simple design is preferable to image overload.

Keep navigation devices constant: The reader should be able to return to the homepage by clicking a banner or icon in the top-left corner, and a site's main sections should be accessible from every other page. Include a contact link in the same place on each page.

Respect Web conventions: Links should stand out, and blue underline is the usual style in text. Main navigation links should change state – colour, underline, roman to bold – when the user hovers over them. Make links clear, but do not use blue underline anywhere non-linking, as it proves too confusing.

Test your site: Do this as your readers might see it, running it across as many browsers as possible and on both Macs and Windows PCs and, if possible, on a range of mobile phones to check its universality.

STAGE-BY-STAGE

A website can take some time to get from the drawing board to the Internet, but the process can be made a lot easier by taking one stage at a time:

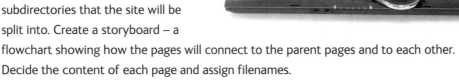

➔ **Purpose:** Identify the purpose of the proposed website. Decide who it is aimed at and what subject matter will be broached. Search the Web for sites covering the same topics or business rivals, and decide how your site will be different. These decisions will help decide the tone of the site's overall design.

➔ **Structure:** Create a basic section structure (see pages 67–69), drawing up a list of the primary sections and subdirectories that the site will be split into. Create a storyboard – a flowchart showing how the pages will connect to the parent pages and to each other. Decide the content of each page and assign filenames.

➔ **Colour and type:** Choose a colour scheme and typefaces. The choice depends on the site's focus and target audience. If it is a business site, choose formal styles, serif fonts and cool shades; hobbyist or personal sites might go for a lighter feel with brighter colours and less austere typefaces.

➔ **Width:** Decide whether you are going to design the page to a fixed width and, if so, which width you should choose. A 1024 x 768-pixel window will display on most monitors without any horizontal scroll, but will you want to risk alienating users of 800 x 600-pixel screens?

⊕ **Template:** Create the basic template, first sketching it out, then transferring your ideas to a web editor (possibly after creating a wireframe outline in a graphics design package). Create the static graphics – the banner, complete with your logo and some basic navigation buttons, for instance – and add them to the template. Transfer the directory structure from the storyboard to the site management section of your web editor.

⊕ **Functionality:** Decide which additional functionality you want to use, such as JavaScript or Flash, and write or download the necessary scripts. Add any over-graphics and apply relative links to your navigation menu.

⊕ **Content:** Write the content for all the pages in a word processor so you can spell-check it before publication. Get a colleague to proofread your work. Feed the new content into the templates and save the pages into the directory structure defined in the original storyboard.

⊕ **Usability:** When all the pages are ready, proof locally or on a closed server for errors. Ask colleagues to check the site's usability. Run an HTML verification tool like HTML Validator (http://www.freehtmlvalidator.com) to check the validity of your code.

⊕ **Availability:** Upload the site to a server and announce its arrival through web directories, search engines and social media sites like Facebook and Twitter.

WEBSITE STRUCTURE

The first step in designing a website is to set out its structure. This governs the site's directory structure, and determines the nature of the navigation system that readers will ultimately see on every page.

Beyond small sites in which all the files sit in one root directory, there are three main types of site structure in widespread use – hierarchical, sequential and grid.

Hierarchical Structure

The hierarchical structure is based on a series of nested directories, all of which stem from the index page in the root directory. The index or homepage links to several section index pages, each of which sits in its own directory and links to a set of topic pages or to third-level directories containing further subsection indexes. The whole structure resembles an inverted family tree, with the branches meeting at the homepage.

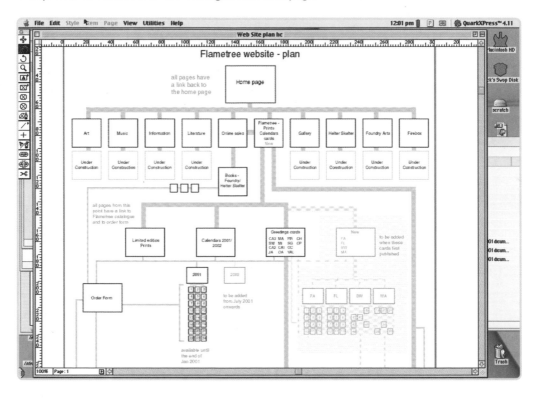

The hierarchical structure's navigation system links every page to its parent and, if applicable, its child page. The main, second-level sections and the homepage should also be accessible from every page. A typical example of the hierarchical structure is a news site that is divided into topics and subtopics.

Sequential Structure

In a sequential structure, pages flow out from the homepage to form a linear narrative. It is usually suited to extended features and tutorials. It is impossible to read page 5, for instance, without having opened pages 1 to 4. The navigation structure of each page merely takes the reader to 'Previous' and 'Next' pages, as well as back Home.

Pages can have additional single pages breaking out from them (to illustrate a tutorial, for instance), but these should form an online cul-de-sac where the only direction is back to the referring page. In such a case, opening a second browser window for these side pages is a neat solution.

Grid Structure

The grid structure is different in that all pages have equal weight and all link to each other. The user can follow any route through the pages, so the content of such a structure has to be well conceived so that each page can stand independent of the others. The grid structure is best used in academic sites, where the reader will already have a basic knowledge of a subject.

When you have decided on a structure, sketch a storyboard showing the links between directories and pages and base your site and navigation system around it. A firm structure is the first step towards offering readers an intuitive, usable website.

FILE ORGANIZATION

Before you start building the pages that will make up your website, decide how you want to store their constituent HTML and image files on the server. If a website consists of fewer than 20 pages, you can safely put them all in the one top-level directory. To preserve order on larger sites, files can be divided into directories based on the site's menu structure. If your site is particularly complex, you can create further subdirectories. Each directory should have an index page (index.htm or equivalent).

Create a separate directory for images at the top level to ease management. Other resources, like Flash animations or movie files, should also be assigned a separate directory.

Linking Files

When referring to files, use relative rather than absolute links. A relative link refers to a second file according to its relationship with the first, for instance, images/banner.gif rather than the absolute http://www.servername.com/images/banner.gif. This makes it easy to move the site wholesale to another server or to a CD.

The best web editors can track changes to a file's name and location, and update all the references to that file across the site. Update the site cache regularly to keep this useful feature running smoothly.

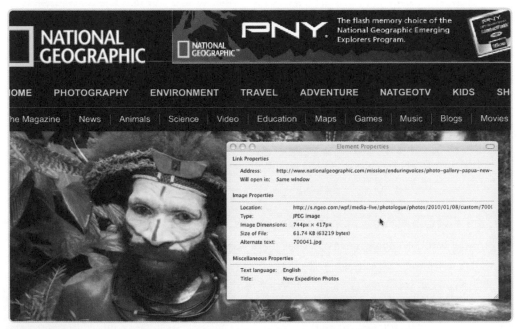

Above: By right-clicking on an image (or using ctrl) and choosing 'Properties', you can see a file's name and location

NAMING CONVENTIONS

It is important when planning your site to take care over the naming of your files to ensure they conform to the naming conventions for your web server's operating system. Each operating system differs in the number of characters it allows in a filename, which characters can be used and whether it is sensitive to uppercase and lowercase letters. For example, a UNIX server is sensitive to case – so a link to Image.gif is not the same as image.gif, while Windows and Mac-based servers are not. Similarly, UNIX servers do not accept spaces in filenames, so links to my file.html will not work, although they will on Windows and Mac servers. Servers are also sensitive to file extensions and the correct one has to be used or the server will not recognize the page.

To avoid any problems, some people adopt the ISO (International Standards Organization) convention for filenames of a maximum of eight letters, followed by a period and a three-letter extension. No spaces or special characters are allowed in names except for the underscore.

GIF OR JPEG?

The overwhelming majority of images on the Web are in one of two formats, GIF and JPEG. The rules that determine when to use one format ahead of the other are clear cut, but many designers seem to pick their favourite image format and use that every time. This can lead to poor image reproduction and unnecessarily long download times.

Compression Types

The key to using the right format is understanding how each is compressed. JPEG is a 'lossy' format, which means that the size of the original high-resolution file is reduced by discarding unnecessary pixels, those parts of the image that the eye is unlikely to miss. If several shades of blue are in close proximity, for instance, a graphics package would replace them with an 'average' blue.

When to Use GIFs

GIFs are compressed by reducing the number of colours in the palette to a maximum of

256 colours (although using a web-safe 216-colour palette when creating GIFs is advisable). By contrast, JPEGs have an unlimited colour palette.

Bearing this in mind, it is better to use GIFs when saving simple, bold vector graphics such as page backgrounds, company logos and menu items, or two- or three-colour text blocks such as buttons and banner headlines. Simple rollover graphics are also more suited to the GIF format, and GIF is the only choice for simple animated graphics – there is no JPEG variant.

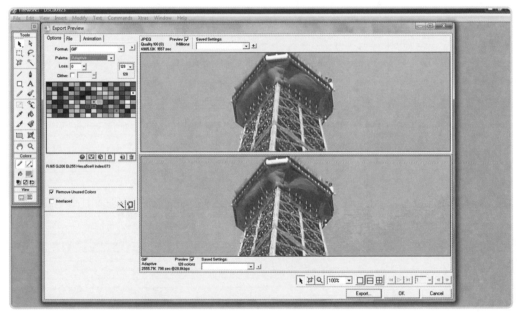

Above: Comparing GIFs and JPEGs

When to Use JPEGs

JPEG is ideal for colourful images such as photographs. You can specify the compression ratio to strike a balance between quality and file size, but bear in mind that smooth graduated areas such as blue skies can break up dramatically at all but the lowest compression levels, and white backgrounds around people can compress to unwanted halos.

When to Use PNGs

A third format, the portable network graphic (PNG), has long been touted as the panacea to the GIF or JPEG problem and, although it is a lossless format, it can be used for photos like JPEGs or for logos like GIFs. PNG files do tend to be larger than their JPEG equivalents, however, although they are smaller than GIF files. Take-up of PNG has not been as widespread as was first hoped.

If you are ever in doubt as to which format to use, all the leading web graphics packages let you preview exported images alongside the original so you can tweak settings and try different formats before committing.

PROPORTIONING PRINCIPLES

Because screen real estate is at a premium, graphics and illustrations on the Web will naturally be smaller than they are in print publications. But, while this lack of detail may disappoint designers, how these graphics are used in relation to each other and to other elements of a web page carries much more importance.

By combining smaller and larger elements on the same page, a clear relationship is created between the items. The user's eye is naturally drawn to a larger element and correctly perceives it to be the more important. This means that the space taken up by more important stories should be larger than for others, and that image-based links to the latest features should be larger than less important links.

Bearing this in mind, do not use a large graphic simply for illustration. It is a waste of screen space and, given the conventions of the Web, a reader may spend time wiping their cursor over it, looking for the phantom link. Instead, consider using the image as a background, although make sure it contrasts suitably with the text or other foreground elements. One solution could be to use the large image as a washed out background with the smaller image in front. This is often used to create eye-catching visual effects in banner advertising.

READABILITY

You can create the best-looking pages on the Web but, if the text content is poor quality, the result could be a visitor-losing embarrassment to your company and yourself.

PRINCIPLES OF READABILITY

There are several points to remember when preparing your website for maximum impact and readability:

➔ **Content is king**: As designers have mastered the standard HTML language, the standards of the English language appear to have gone out the window, and the kind of errors that would never reach a printing press are commonplace on the Web. In fact, checking spelling and grammar is as important as checking valid hyperlinks and image

Above & right: Examples of websites with good readability

references. Always create content in a word processor and get someone else to proofread it before publication.

Keep text blocks narrow: Long lines of text are difficult to read, so each line should include no more than 12 words. Use a fixed-width design to keep the width of paragraphs to 400 pixels at most.

Short and sweet: Long paragraphs are a turn-off, and six lines is a realistic maximum. HTML paragraphing inserts line breaks to add white space to a page, and this spacing can be increased – and readability enhanced – by using bold or coloured subheads every few paragraphs.

Simple and effective: Do not use too many typefaces on a page. Use one font for paragraph text and one for headings. You are not tied to using serif fonts for the main text as you are with print and, in fact, sans serif fonts such as Arial or Verdana are easier to read on-screen.

Check alignment: Left-aligned text is the only sensible option for paragraphs as it gives the reader a constant starting point when they return to the start of the next line. Centred text is fine for single lines such as headlines, while right-aligned text works if it is anchored to a sharp-edge, such as when used for a picture caption or section header.

Easy on the eye: Make sure the text contrasts with the background. Black on white is best for paragraphs and, if you must use light text on dark colour, embolden the text to make it more readable.

Anti-aliasing: When creating text as a graphic for small buttons or section headers, switch off anti-aliasing (see page 128) in your graphics package, as smaller blocks of text can blur to the point of illegibility when it is applied. For larger blocks of image-based text, use anti-aliasing to avoid it becoming blocky and equally unreadable.

TYPOGRAPHY

The rules for specifying fonts for the web are similar to print publishing, except that you cannot be sure what fonts are installed on the destination system. Fortunately, cascading style sheets (CSS) are giving the designer more control.

Proportions

The small proportions of the browser window mean the dramatic differences in font size in print publishing are nonexistent. Rather than using a 50–100-point difference between headline and body fonts, web designers only have a maximum headline size of around 36 points, so colour must be used to make the headline stand out.

Resolution

On high-resolution screens, line lengths can be too long to follow comfortably across the page. The <blockquote> tag sets a narrow paragraph width, but it is better to set the text in a fixed-width table or specify where each line ends using the <br> line break tab at the end of each line.

Size

Font sizes in HTML are relative (3 being the standard, 7 the largest), but users can choose larger or smaller fonts according to their own taste. Use cascading style sheets to set precise sizes. CSS lets you specify font and line spacing sizes in pixels, points, ems and metric measures.

Fonts

Because the type size tends to be larger on the Web, the print convention of using serif fonts for body text and sans-serif fonts for headlines and other one-line page furniture does not apply online, and most sites now use a sans-serif font throughout.

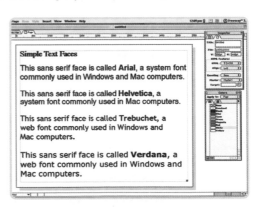

Arial (Windows) and Helvetica (Mac) are the most popular sans-serif fonts online because they are installed on most PCs, but consider using a typeface designed especially for the Web such as Verdana or Trebuchet MS. Do not italicize fonts, as the square pixel grid will create a jagged effect.

Case

Print rules regarding upper and lower case still apply, and you should use mixed case as much as possible. All upper case stands out too much and, on the Web, is seen as the written form of shouting, while all lower case in body text and headlines looks like grammatical ineptitude.

SPACING

How you use white space in web design is as important as how you use colour. Spacing between page elements can add extra emphasis to the content and helps guide the reader's eye around the page. While reading, the eye strays towards white space; if all it can see is a solid block of text or tightly packed images, it will skirt over the content looking for the space.

Words of Warning

However, this does not mean you should overload a site with white space at the expense of content, and getting the balance right is essential. If your page is organized into a three-column grid, for example, separate the columns slightly using the cellpadding or cellspacing table attributes. This gives a clear definition between the columns, but apply a padding of no more than 25 pixels or the columns will be too far apart and will lose their connection. Similarly, you can use the cellpadding attributes to put a small white 'border' around the most important blocks of text.

Images should also be set as islands of white space. The 'vspace' and 'hspace' attributes place additional space around two sides of an image, or you can use the single-pixel GIF trick to add space to just one side of the image and preserve alignment with other elements.

COLOURS AND SHAPES

The colours and shapes you choose to use on your website can make it smart and impactful or send your viewer into a web of confusion, at best having trouble identifying your brand and at worst unable to easily read and follow your message.

COLOUR CODES

In converting their talents to the Web, designers accustomed to the four-colour CMYK (Cyan, Magenta, Yellow and blacK) print process have to get to grips with the three-colour RGB (Red, Green, Blue) concept used by computers.

RGB v. CMYK

Specifying the red, green and blue values of on-screen colours works the opposite way to picking a CMYK colour. The cyan, magenta, yellow and black values represent the amount of ink on a page, so 100 per cent magenta and 100 per cent yellow produces a warm red, with no cyan or black ink on the page. With the RGB mode, however, you have to specify the amount of red, green and blue light that is projected on screen. Thus a warm red would require a maximum red value of 255, and green and blue values of zero.

Hex Code

Colours within HTML pages or cascading style sheets (CSS) have to be specified not by their RGB values, but in hexadecimal code. Hex code, or base-16, runs from 00 (zero) to FF (255), and the Calculator accessory on the Windows Start Menu will convert these values for you. Alternatively, several design websites, including the Web Building section at www.builder.com, have colour code converters. You simply type in the decimal value of each element of the colour and the converter displays the hex code, along with a panel which fills with your chosen colour – a useful precaution in case you should get a number wrong.

Specifying Colours

When specifying a colour in HTML, you need to include the hash sign in front of the six-character value. For instance, if you were specifying a bright yellow background for a page, the code <body bg colour="#FFFF00"> tells the browser that it should mix maximum red and green (FF) with no blue (00). Note that there are no spaces or commas between the three colour values.

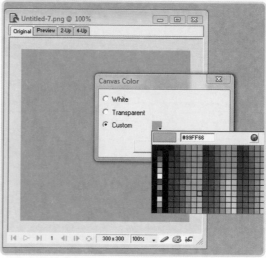

Above: Specifying colour codes

Fortunately, you can also specify colours by name, and some 140 named colours – all of which are web-safe – have been specified. These run from the basic red, green, blue, black and white through simple variations such as navy blue and sky blue to almost abstract shades like 'peru' and 'papayawhip'. Our example, then, would read <body bg colour="yellow">.

If you do use named colours rather than hex RGB code, make a note of its RGB values as you may want to replicate the colour in an inline graphic where you will need to enter the RGB values into your graphics package.

WEB-SAFE COLOURS

Because of differences in the specifications of PCs and Macintosh systems, and in a bid to meet the realistic lowest common denominator of 256-colour graphics subsystems, only 216 colours can be certain of appearing identically on all computer systems. Web editors and graphics design programs can be locked to use web-safe colours, and you should use only web-safe colours where possible.

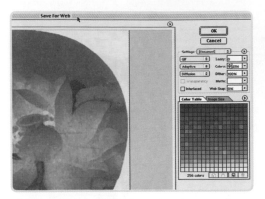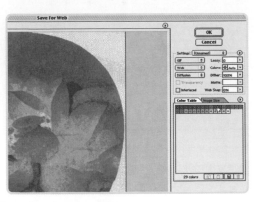

Above: Saving a GIF file from the adaptive palette to the web–safe colour palette

Colour Palettes

The palette size of 216 colours is a result of accident rather than design. The first colour PCs
and Macintosh systems only had 8-bit graphics subsystems with a limited amount of memory,
and so could display only 256 colours at most. All other colours would have to be created by
combinations of these 256 using a technology called dithering (*see* page 44). When choosing
which 256 colours should be displayed without dithering, however, the major computer
platform developers disagreed slightly, and only 216 colours remained common to the basic
palettes of PCs and Macs.

Palettes

Web-safe palette charts can be viewed online at sites such as www.web-source.net/216
_color_chart.htm, and one look at the hex codes of each colour will give a clue as to how the
palette was created. The web-safe palette only contains RGB values of 0, 20 per cent, 40 per
cent, 60 per cent, 80 per cent and 100 per cent of 255, that is to say only red, green and blue
values of 0 (00 in hex), 51 (33), 102 (66), 153 (99), 204 (CC) and 255 (FF) are used. If you are
entering hex codes manually, colours based on values outside these six will not be web-safe.

Applying Web-safe Colours

It is not necessary to use web-safe colours at all times. Photographs saved as JPEGs, for instance, will degrade when a web-safe palette is applied, and the dithering involved will probably push the file size up, as well.

Simple GIFs should always be created from the web-safe palette, especially where expanses of one or two colours are concerned – what looks like a sea of red on your Macintosh screen could become a swamp of brown when the page is opened on a PC. Small blocks of text – saved as GIFs or generated by HTML – should also be web safe, as dithering could render the type unreadable on older monitors. The three or four main components of your site's colour scheme should always be referred to by their web-safe hex codes to ensure consistency.

COLOUR WHEELS

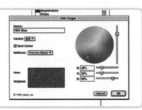

A colour wheel gives designers a visual representation of the colours available to them. All graphics design packages let you access colour wheels to select a colour and, while they should be combined with a web-safe colour palette to make sure you pick suitable colours, wheels expose relationships between colours that can be used to enhance the design of your site.

Above: RGB colour wheel

Viewing the Spectrum

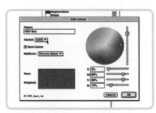

Wheels come in both RGB and CMYK models, but for web design you will be using the RGB/HSL (*see* page 82) model. A colour wheel is essentially a spectrum wrapped into a circle, with the primary additive (light-based) colours – red, green and blue – set every 120 degrees on the perimeter. In between the primary colours are the secondary colours, produced when the primaries are combined (red and green producing yellow, blue and red making violet and green and blue combining to form light blue). Then there are the tertiary colours, produced by combining each primary colour with its adjacent secondary colours.

Above: CMYK colour wheel

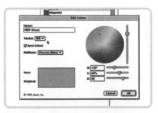

Above: HSL colour wheel

Hue and Brightness

These 12 basic colours are called the hues and form the basic colour wheel. In the more complex wheels found in graphics packages, the amount of white added to each hue increases towards the centre of the wheel. By adding more white, the hue's saturation decreases to create tints of the original colour.

Independent to the colour wheel is the brightness (or luminosity) setting. By decreasing the brightness of a hue, you are effectively adding degrees of grey and then black to the original, to create tones and shades. Good colour combinations can be created by combining a tint, a tone and a shade of a hue with the original.

Colour Measurements

As well as an RGB reading, good colour wheels will also display a reading for the hue, saturation and luminosity/brightness (HSL or HSB). Hue is valued between zero and 0.999, while saturation and luminosity are rated between zero and 1.000. While you will only need to make a note of this if you are adding colours to Java applets, understanding how altering hue, saturation and light can affect a colour is the key to selecting suitable and complementary colours for your site.

COLOUR COMBINATIONS

Almost all printed documents use dark text on a white background but, just because the Web gives easy access to thousands of colours, do not try to use as many as you can all at once. Web designers understand this, and more sensible, legible colour combinations have replaced the somewhat garish designs witnessed during the early days of the Web.

Contrast

When choosing a colour scheme for the text-heavy areas of your site, contrast is crucial. Black on white is the obvious solution, but if you want to add colour, dark blues, greens or reds make for legible text on white or light backgrounds. Combining dark and light shades of the same colour is a common solution. But, while they make good headline colours, resist the temptation to use bright colours for text, as this could be hard to read continuously for any length of time. Avoid light text on dark backgrounds as, again, this can be difficult to read for more than a paragraph. Even where light on dark is acceptable, for example, for menu panels, straplines or boxouts (boxes containing extra information, separate to the main body of text), use a bold typeface to make the text stand out.

Background Colours

With pictorial backgrounds, try to lighten the background image so that text is still legible over the top of it. Black text is often your only option here. For graphics, legibility will be less important, but the dangers of mismatching colours are no less prevalent. The eye is a good indicator of which colours complement each other and which clash, but you can get a fair idea by using a colour wheel. Using an RGB colour wheel, adjacent colours, for instance, red and yellow or green and light blue, are said to be complementary and can offer a good contrast between light and dark.

Above: Choosing text and background colour

Saturated Colours

As we have seen, you can change the saturation or brightness of a colour by adding more white, grey or black to the original hue; so a good way of creating effective colour combinations is to select a fully saturated colour and combine it with a variety of tints, tones and shades of the same colour. Specifying three hues that are side-by-side on a colour wheel is good for creating a thematic effect. A saturated red, orange and yellow, for instance, presents a sunny disposition, while shades of these three colours adds an earthy feel. Tints of blue, green and light blue, meanwhile, create a cold but calming effect.

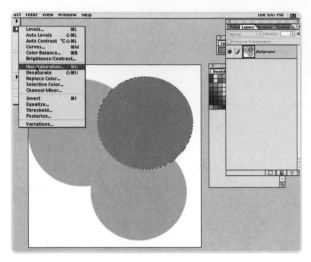

Three colours that are equidistant on a wheel, or their tints, tones and shades, work surprisingly well together. Generally, a good rule of thumb when specifying colour schemes using a colour wheel is to keep two of the hue, saturation and light settings constant across the three or four colours you select.

Left: Combining a fully saturated colour with tints, tones and shades

Pitfalls

When combining colours, however, do consider colour-blind PC users. Do not combine any two of red, green, brown, grey or purple in an image, and insist on a strong contrast between foreground and background colours. If possible, switch to a greyscale setting and see how legible your website is. If it proves difficult to read, try a more contrasting combination.

MONITOR CALIBRATION

Calibration differences mean that colours viewed on one monitor look different when viewed on another. The differences are not only from computer to computer, but also from platform to platform.

At the end of the day, your web pages will be viewed on screen, and even if everything else was perfectly compatible, colours on one monitor are going to look different to colours on another. Not only is it the type of monitor or video card that makes the difference, it is also the number of colours it supports, the resolution at which it is viewed and the level of gamma correction (that is, the overall brightness).

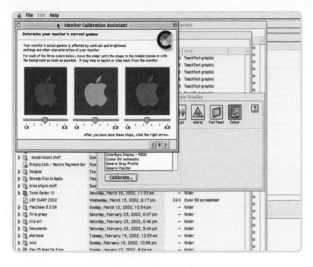

Left: Assessing the level of gamma correction

Gamma Difference

Even in design companies, few monitors are calibrated accurately to one another, with the result that shades of colour look drastically different on different machines. The differences are not only noticeable between the different platforms but also between individual PCs.

Particularly noticeable as a cross-platform issue is the gamma difference. Gamma levels control the brightness and contrast of your computer monitor, but they are set differently on the Mac to the PC or UNIX. As a result, images generally appear darker on the Mac, while those taken from a PC appear washed out on a Mac.

GEOMETRIC SHAPES

Just as primary colours are the basic building blocks when using colour, so designers should master use of the basic geometric shapes before working on the overall layout of a website. Linear shapes are uninteresting and do not draw the reader's eye in, but lines, circles, rectangles and ellipses can be combined to make an inviting, engaging homepage. There are several points to remember when using geometric shapes in design.

⊖ **Straight lines:** The most basic geometric shape is the straight line. HTML's own horizontal rule <hr> tag lets you break up paragraphs with lines, but its own default style lacks something in form. The standard rule is a bevelled line which, while applying a 3D effect to the page, is probably out of keeping with your site's design. Fortunately, the

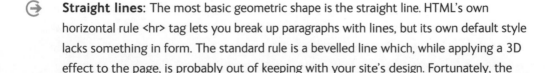

'noshade' variable flattens the rule and a 'color=' attribute lets you tie its colour in with the overall scheme of your page. Run each rule as a percentage of a cell width so that it does not slice the page into stark rectangles.

Vertical lines: These can apply an overly rigid grid effect to a page and should also be used sparingly. In graphical terms, however, they can be used, especially when combined with horizontal lines to form crosses, to draw the reader into the most important part of the page. Eyes naturally follow lines, and lines can be used to coax a reader around the page from item to item. Adding an arrowhead or a bullet to the line enhances this effect.

Rectangles: Given that every PC screen is rectangular, it is no surprise that rectangles are so common in web design. Increased use of table-based design means that pages tend to be divided into shaded boxes, which neither please the eye nor encourage movement around the page.

Right angles: Play down the impression of a page full of right angles by not shading boxes and increasing the cellpadding attribute of the <table> tag to create some space around the text. White space also emphasizes the content.

Round corners: Round-cornered rectangles are less austere than right-angled boxes. Use them to hold large blocks of contents, such as menus.

Graduated fills: These can help lose the impression of a rectangle by blending an object such as a page header with the rest of the page.

Coloured rectangles: Mixing rectangles of different colours and applying borders of different weights on a page can be eye-catching, provided you include plenty of white space in between to create a non-linear effect.

→ **Complete circles**: These are rare on the Web, as all elements of HTML are essentially quadrilateral, and full circles are not ideal placeholders outside splash screens. Their linearity also makes them less eye-catching than ellipses.

→ **Semicircles**: Coloured half- and semicircles in the inside corners of rectangles help to break up the linearity of the right angles. Similarly, light ellipses act as good page and table backgrounds.

→ **Lozenges**: A semicircle added to the end of a rectangle creates a good lozenge effect for dynamic-looking menu items, while quarter-circles can smooth the corners of boxes.

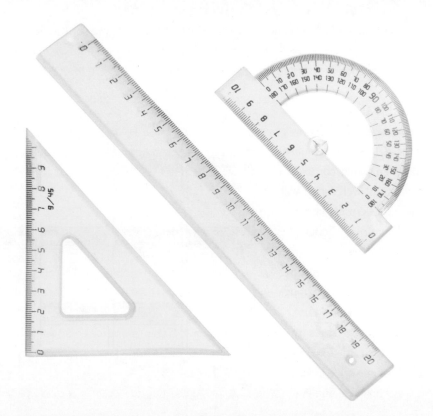

UNDERSTANDING BROWSERS

Understanding how browsers work is key to getting your website right. What looks great on your own browser might look completely different on someone else's. Although in the past compatibility was a big issue, today most browsers work in a similar way to each other and there are easy ways of ensuring compatibility.

CROSS-BROWSER COMPATIBILITY

Despite the best efforts of the World Wide Web Consortium (W3C) to set standards that all software manufacturers should adhere to, not all browsers display a web page in the same way. To maximize your audience, ensure that pages are compatible with the most popular browsers.

Problems in the Past

There are over 200 browsers available for PC, Mac, PDA, mobile phone and even games consoles, but 95 per cent of web surfers will be using either Microsoft Internet Explorer (IE), Firefox or Google's Chrome. Not that this concentration makes the task any easier – versions dating back four or five years could still be in use, and there are platform issues to consider, with the same browsers displaying the same code in very different ways on Macs and PCs.

Above: Testing a website across different versions of several browsers

Above: There are various websites that offer cross–browser compatibility checking tools, such as http://browsershots.org and www.browsercam.com

Updated Browsers

Fortunately, after much incompatibility, the latest versions of IE, Firefox and Chrome are almost identical in the way they work with HTML, although there are still slight discrepancies in CSS, DHTML, XML and ActiveX support. Font sizes, the dimensions of form elements and spacing also vary slightly between editions. But it is in the use of older browsers where problems occur, and you have to compromise your use of CSS for design and positioning so that elements are positioned identically in all versions of all browsers – the padding and margin properties can mean very different things to older versions of IE and Firefox.

Taking Precautions

For realistic cross-browser support, try to comply with version 6.0 of IE and version 2.5 of Firefox, and check the page in as many browsers as possible as often as possible. This poses problems as well, though, since IE does not react well to sharing hard-disk space with older versions. The only solution is to install the older version on to a clean machine, or ask colleagues (not forgetting the Mac users) to check the site's appearance for you. Firefox is a little more understanding, and you can install multiple versions of Navigator, provided they are in different directories.

Finally, test as often as possible and clean up the code if necessary. Dreamweaver's Target Browser Check will look over your page and report any compatibility problems. Really, though, there is no substitute for testing your site in the browsers themselves.

TECHNICAL LIMITATIONS

The Web is not like other media; unlike print publishing, when you build a site, you do not know how it is going to appear on the reader's system. A high-spec system will be able to display all the streaming video clips you want, but users of older PCs will miss out on such cutting-edge content. Good web design is all about catering for the realistic lowest common denominator. The current lowest acceptable screen size is 800 x 600 pixels, and you can meet this limitation by designing to a fixed width of 760 pixels. A user of a low-spec system might have a depth of only 256 colours, and adhering to the web-safe palette of 216 colours is always good practice.

Not all users will be equipped with the latest browsers, so check your page on older browsers and try not to use standards that are only supported by certain browsers. Also avoid using non-standard technologies that require new plug-ins: users would rather not wait to see content, however inspiring.

Access Speeds

Consider the user's access speeds. Although broadband access is widespread, the speed of that broadband varies – do not assume that everyone will have a 20 MBit line. To make sure your page loads as quickly as possible, make sure you do not overload a page with graphics, and keep the size of both page and images reasonably small. If you use Flash or Java elements for navigation, try not to use more than one element per page as these take longer to download.

FUNCTIONALITY

Despite constant advances, by its definition as a mark-up language, HTML is mainly concerned with the appearance of web pages rather than true interactivity with the reader. Using additional tools and server-side software, it is possible to tailor a site to individual users, react dynamically to reader input and interact with database content to offer search, message boards and e-commerce tools.

```
        if (target=="")
                tgt = window;
        else if (target=="_parent")
                tgt = window.parent;
        else if (target=="_top")
                tgt = window.top;
        else if (window[target])
                tgt = window[target];
        else if (window.top[target])
                tgt = window.top[target];
        else
        {
                window.top.open(link, target);
                return;
        }

        tgt.location = link;
}

function FWRandom()
{
        fwRnd.seed = (fwRnd.seed*fwRnd.a+fwRnd.c)%fwRnd.m;
        return fwRnd.seed/fwRnd.m;
}
var fwRnd=new Object;
fwRnd.m=714025;fwRnd.a=4096;fwRnd.c=150889;
fwRnd.seed = (new Date()).getTime()%fwRnd.m;

function FWRandomInt(max,last)
{
        if (max < 2) return max;
        var result = Math.floor(FWRandom()*max-1)+1;
        while(last && result == last)
                result = Math.floor(FWRandom()*max-1)+1;
        return result;
}
function RandomLink(){var rnd=FWRandomInt(20,document.fwRandomLink);document.fwRandomLi
nd==1)link="haikujoy.html";if (rnd==2)link="haikuspirit.html";if (rnd==3)link="haikuten:
//-->
</SCRIPT></HEAD><BODY TOPMARGIN=0 LEFTMARGIN=0 MARGINHEIGHT=0 MARGINWIDTH=0 BGCOLOR="#F
VALIGN=MIDDLE><IMG SRC="resources/bamboocut1bar.gif" BORDER=0 WIDTH=314 HEIGHT=89 ALT=""
```

Above: JavaScript for a random link

JavaScript Routines

The most common way of extending a browser's functionality is to use JavaScript routines. While often used to create image rollovers and visual effects, JavaScript is ideal for small personalization tasks – detecting where the user is based and adding their local time to a page, for instance. It is also suited to small calculations and form verification, such as for checking that a credit-card booking form has been completed correctly.

CGI Scripts

Most current server-side functionality will be in the form of CGI scripts, usually written in Perl or C, or Active Server Pages (ASP). There are thousands of CGI scripts available to buy online (as well as less stable free scripts) for building shopping carts, password protection, online auction systems, searches, guestbooks and polls. ASP pages perform the same functions as CGI scripts, but use Visual Basic-style tools.

WEBSITE MAINTENANCE

Designing and publishing a website is only the start of the work. Once a site is uploaded and has started pulling in readers, the work of keeping the site up-to-date and running smoothly really begins. An out-of-date website full of broken links has little credibility and will soon start leaking visitors.

BASIC MAINTENANCE

There are several key points to remember about your website once it is up and running:

- **Update information:** The instant nature of web publishing means that few websites are truly up to date, as there is always new information to be added. The subject matter of some sites lends itself more to regular updates than other topics, but take a look at a rival site and try to update as often as they do.

- **Update links:** If you have no new content to post on the site, make the most of your initial hard work and feature links to different permanent areas of the site from the front page. Many users may not have discovered those sections and a simple button will make it look as though you have added a new section.

- **Update the date:** All websites are 'under construction', so avoid using the phrase and don't upload sections unless they are complete. If you think a site will not be updated very often, don't put a 'Last updated ...' notice on the site. Instead, you can add a simple JavaScript that displays today's date automatically.

- **Check external links:** Check any external links at least once a month. Sites can be taken down or their URLs changed, and Not Found links look sloppy.

Check functionality: Run regular checks to ensure your own site is working properly and that all links and images are valid using a diagnostic tool like Google's Webmaster Tools.

Get feedback: Get users' feedback about the site and respond with words and actions. Feedback could be through emails or contact forms, through surveys (available through sites such as Sparklit.com) or through the site's own message board. Contribute to the board to help build and maintain the community and always respond to emails personally, and not with a computer-generated message.

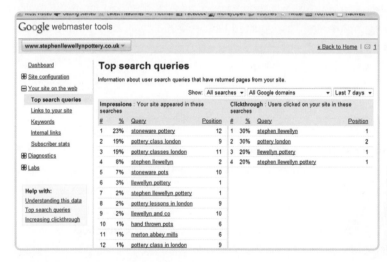

Left: Google Webmaster Tools. Sites such as these provide you with detailed reports about your site's visibility on the Web

Check site logs: Monitor the site logs using tools from Google Analytics, webstat.com or GoStats.com. These will tell you a lot about how users read the site, and which pages are most popular. You can then prioritize sections to update ahead of others.

Redesign if necessary: HTML is always evolving, so consider redesigning the site every 18–24 months, starting from scratch. Adapt older content to the new design and do not take the old site down for a day or two before relaunching.

MAINTAINING WEBSITE INTEREST

Whether a site is created to promote a business or to share one's leisure interests with the world, webmasters like to see healthy visitor numbers. And whether those are in the hundreds or the millions, the site owner will want the figures to continue climbing. As well as creating interesting and diverting content, there is a lot webmasters can do to keep visitors coming back.

Updating Your Site

Regular updates are vital. The Web has become the first port of call for users seeking the latest information and news, and your site will soon be overlooked if the most interesting thing on the front page is a legend reading 'Last updated January 2008'. This is even more important for corporate sites, where images of long-retired chief executives and outdated phone numbers will not only turn visitors away from your site, but will lose you business.

Promoting Your Website

To make the most of any updates, why not shout about it by listing and linking to the newly updated areas on the front page? Visitors will not only be able to find the freshest content quickly, they will also be impressed by the topicality of the site and are more likely to return regularly.

You can promote your new content for free using social networking sites such as Twitter, or by setting up a Facebook 'fan' page for your site and posting links to popular pages there.

Mailing Lists

You can take this a degree further by sending out daily or weekly updates to subscribers using list management software such as PHPlist (http://www.phplist.com/). After installing the software on your server, webmasters can then send out an email to thousands of users at once, announcing site updates and featuring links back to the site. The trick here, especially if you are running a news-based site, is not to send out entire stories, but teaser paragraphs that will tempt the subscribers back to the site.

Left: PHPList newsletter manager is one way of reminding users of your site

User Contributions

Sometimes, there may be no new content to upload, at which point why not let the readers add to the site's content themselves? A lot of websites host chat forums and message boards which webmasters can customize to their own page design, and not worry about managing or hosting the site. Users will also return time and again to monitor topical polls. Sparklit (www.sparklit.com) and Alxnet (www.alxnet.com) offer free polls and quizzes that can be incorporated into the design of any site and, again, packaged poll solutions are available for business sites.

Added Value

Entertainment is another winning formula. If you have the talent and the resources, basic games created in Flash or Shockwave can keep visitors coming back, especially if you can add a high-score leaderboard to keep the challenge going. Competition prizes – no matter how small – also draw users back.

Finally, spread the word about your site. Regular users will download and install branded screensavers and desktop wallpaper, and this might catch the eye of friends or office colleagues. Businesses should advertise their URL on all stationery, and have enough diverting content on the site to keep visitors coming back time and again.

WEB STANDARDS

HTML standards are recommended by the World Wide Web Consortium (W3C) for browser developers, web software companies and developers to follow. W3C now recommends standards for HTML, XHTML, CSS and XML, as well as a host of less important web technologies.

W3C RECOMMENDATIONS

W3C makes its recommendations after a lengthy consultation process that begins when one of the organization's members – which include the computer industry's biggest corporations – makes a submission for a new standard. W3C's working group then produces a series of drafts until the final version is recommended to the industry.

Web standards are designed to be both backwards-compatible and forwards-compatible. Pages conforming to older recommendations should appear error-free on future browsers, while sites based on future standards should at least display their core content on older browsers. Other standards in development at the W3C are cascading style sheets (CSS), XML and XSL.

Validation

Even if you intend writing to a W3C standard, your web-editing software might not be (FrontPage, for example, favours some IE extensions), so have a copy of the HTML standards to hand and run a site through an HTML checker to trace any non-standard elements. The W3C has its own online page validator at http://validator.w3.org/ which checks your code, and an additional CSS validator at http://jigsaw.w3.org/css-validator/.

Above: W3C web standards online page validator

REACHING ALL USERS

Just as all good websites should work correctly across as many browsers as possible, so they should be accessible to as many users as possible, and that means complying with accessibility guidelines. For personal websites, this is merely advisable, but for corporate sites, it is a legal requirement.

The DDA

The UK's Disability Discrimination Act (DDA) makes it unlawful for any service provider to discriminate against a disabled person by refusing to provide any service which it provides to members of the public. When this applies to websites, it means that a site must be specially designed so that users with visual impairments can read the site and use any interactive tools – for example, online purchasing systems – via a browser add-on called a screen reader. As its name suggests, a screen reader reads the content of your page aloud in a default order – main (h1) headings first, then secondary (h2) headings and so on, right down to the text. Images are either ignored or the 'alt' text read out.

Following Guidelines

A full checklist of accessibility guidelines, drawn up by the World Wide Web Consortium, can be found at http://www.w3.org/TR/WAI-WEBCONTENT/full-checklist.html, but there are some basic accessibility rules that all web designers should follow:

- **Provide accurate and appropriate 'alt' text for all images, including image maps**
- **Use a correct heading structure, using the h1, h2, h3, etc hierarchy**
- **Produce accessible and well-written page content**
- **Use predefined styles for both formatting and layout effects**
- **Insert table headers into data tables – use the <th> tags**

Using CSS – and specifically the 'em' value rather than the pixel or point measurements – makes it easier for the reader to resize text on a page according to their own requirements. Many sites include a small control panel at the top of the screen which lets the user change font size at the touch of a button. Some offer high-contrast text display or different colour schemes.

BASIC WEB DESIGN

CREATING A BASIC WEB PAGE

Below is all the basic information you need to get started – make sure you understand the principles of basic web design before you get going, otherwise you'll spend hours undoing careless work

STARTING OUT

The document markup language HTML is used to build web pages. It tells the browser how to display what is on the page. It also contains the links that connect one document to another. All HTML documents are collections of tags, enclosed within less than (<) and greater than (>) brackets. Most are also container tags, that is they have an opening tag (such as <i>) and a closing tag (</i>). The tags tell the browser how to display anything that is contained within the tags. So, <i> this text is shown in italic </i>. While HTML will still display some content that does not have closing tags, XHTML (eXtensible Hypertext Markup Language – the latest generation of HTML) is less forgiving and end tags will be needed.

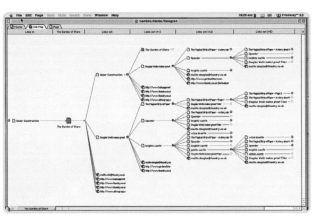

Above: A site map is a very useful way of keeping track of your design, showing links within the site and to other websites.

Modifying Tags

Tags can be modified by attributes, stated in the opening tag, which allow you to specify properties such as font, size, colour, etc. So, <font colour="#FF0000"> puts the text in red. In HTML, if an attribute has a value, that is a single word or number, it does not need to go between quote marks, but XHTML does require all attributes to go in quotes.

Above: A graphic approach to web design, by an application such as Freeway, can allow you to create links and see how the site will look in a browser without an intimate knowledge of html

Similarly, HTML itself is not sensitive to case – so <FONT> is the same as <font>. However, XHTML is case sensitive and all tags need to be in lower case. In preparation for that it is as well to start coding tags in lower case anyway.

Document Parts

Each HTML document has two main parts, the <head>, which contains general information about the file and scripts that need to be run, and the <body>, which is the content that will appear in the browser window. Normally, this HTML outline for the page will be automatically set up by your web-authoring program. Typically, the page will start with a document type definition which lets the browser know which HTML standard you are following. Within the head, you should also include the <title>, which has the text that will appear in the browser's title bar (e.g. <title>Web Design Greats</title>).

Margins and Colours

By default, most browsers leave several pixels of space around the web page. If you want your page flush to the top and left of the browser window, you need to set the page margins. In Internet Explorer, set topmargin and leftmargin attributes to zero. For Firefox, use the same setting in marginheight and marginwidth.

Add a splash of colour to the background by using the 'bgcolor' attribute in the <body> tag. If you want to get jazzy, add a background image that tiles, that is repeats, across the viewable area. To do this, add 'background' as the attribute to the <body> tag and also enter the file location for the image. Beware that the background does not make it too difficult to read the text on the page.

Checking Content

Content may not be king on all websites, but it does need treating royally. Ensure that any content is as sharp and short as possible and free of grammatical or spelling mistakes. Design-wise, you can do a lot to help get the message across. For spacing, the paragraph tag <p>...</p> adds additional white space when it breaks the line. If you do not want the extra space use the line-break tag <br>, which is also one of the few standalone tags that does not have an end tag. You can add emphasis to text with the italic or bold tags.

Headings and Images

For greater visual emphasis, add headings to the page. There are six available, <h1> being the biggest and <h6> the smallest (too small for most viewers). With most browsers, <h4> is equivalent to the size of the body text. The typeface, size and colour can all be set through the <font> tag, but this is gradually being phased out in favour of using style sheets. However, it is still needed to work with older browsers.

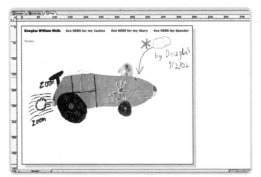 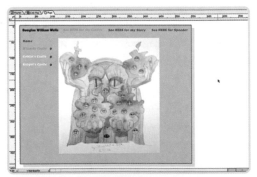

Above: Simple navigation and a direct approach to graphic design can be very effective for children's sites

For visual interest, add images to the web page using the standalone <img> tag followed by the 'src' attribute with the location of the graphics file. By using the 'height' and 'width' attributes to specify the actual pixel size of the image, you effectively insert a placeholder which preserves the layout as the page is downloaded. For those who have disabled image downloading, or who have non-graphical browsers, you should also use the 'alt' attribute to provide a brief textual description of the image.

Spacing

Using the 'vspace' and 'hspace' attributes, you can add extra space between text and graphics but for more precise alignment it is best to use tables. A table is created with the opening and closing <table> tags followed by one or more table rows <tr>. Within each row, there are data cells that use the <td> tag. By putting text or images within the data cells, you can help structure the page more clearly and control the layout more precisely.

To really connect to the Web, you can create hyperlinks from either your graphics or text. Select the object you want to link and use the anchor tag <a> with the 'href' attribute followed by the address (URL) of the page you are linking to. This can either be absolute for an external link (one outside your site), including the protocol and domain name (e.g. http://www.expedia.com), or relative for files on the same server.

META TAGS

These document information tags are a way of including information about a document and the content it contains that is particularly used by search engines to describe and categorize web pages. Meta tags, which must be nested inside the head of a web page, hold hidden information about the document. Invisible to the reader, this is picked up by servers, browsers or search engines and acted on.

Tag Types

There are two main types of tag, the 'http-equiv' and 'name'. Information provided by 'http-equiv' generally affects the way your browser deals with a document. So it can be used to reload a page after a certain time delay (in which case it would be linked to information that is being updated by the server) or to redirect users to a different URL.

Above: Meta tag information for Microsoft's website

The 'name' attribute normally contains information about the content of the page, such as the author's name and details of the copyright as well as two tags – description and keyword – that are used by many search engines for categorizing and indexing documents.

Text put within the description tag describes the content of your web page. If the tag is recognized by the search engine, the description will appear on the search results page. As some engines only display around 20-word descriptions, you need to put the important information early on. With the keyword tag, you can provide a comma-separated list of words to help search engines index your document.

PAGE LAYOUT

Web page layout has come a long way from the early days, when each element lined up left in the window, one under another. Today, it can be an immense multimedia experience that, at its best, can rival TV. And this evolution has taken place in a relatively short period of time.

Style Sheets

HTML's table tags and cascading style sheets (CSS) have added tools for creating grids that can align objects and include the designer's best friend – white space. The arrival of style sheets has meant that designers also have much fuller control over the look and feel of a page. Along the way, some tags have been lost – such as Netscape's <blink> for blinking text – but generally the designer has gained a lot more. For instance, table tags, originally designed to hold traditional statistical data, have been adapted; now they hold text, graphics, even other nested tables, and are a powerful way to break up a page both horizontally and vertically. Tables also provide a basic design grid similar to, although less flexible than, page layout programs such as InDesign.

Style sheets provide a centrally stored set of definitions for different layout attributes, such as text size, line spacing or indents. A single definition can be applied site-wide, so changes can be done in one hit rather than being applied to each specific instance.

As a layout tool, CSS treats each element as an object, or box. So, rather like the table cell, you can add a background colour, borders, extra padding, etc. With CSS positioning, you can also tell the browser the exact place on screen that you want the box placed. This can either be a pixel-precise co-ordinate (absolute) or relative to some other box or the top left of the browser (relative). It is this positioning that is at the heart of DHTML and can be used with JavaScript for animation and interactivity.

DESIGNING FOR DIFFERENT RESOLUTIONS

In designing for the Web, it is important to bear in mind that users will be viewing your pages at various sizes. Given people's reluctance to scroll, particularly horizontally, it is important to try to fit your page within the likely screen size of most of your visitors. Fortunately, the growth of screens in recent years means you have plenty of pixels to work with but, even though most users view 1024 x 768 or 1280 x 800 screens, some people may be restricted to using screens of 800 x 600 pixels. If you want to cater for these, design a flexible layout by setting the width of the whole page to 100 per cent, fixing the width of any vertical columns on the extreme left and right of the page, and leave the central section without a width value. That way, your page will expand widthways to fill the browser window.

SITE LAYOUT (USING TABLES)

Tables can be both a great aid and a great nuisance. They offer a good way to clearly structure the page layout and are useful to control alignment, but the HTML can be very confusing when tables are nested within each other. It can also be a headache to remember which table elements are controlled at the table level and which at the cell level.

For the overall page structure, tables can be used to create the major sections. For instance, a left-hand column could house the navigation buttons while the main column has the content. The width of the table can either be fixed (each column is a precise number of pixels) or relative (where they are resized relative to the width of the window). To achieve this, the table width is set to 100 per cent and each column is a percentage of this. Tables can also be a combination of fixed and relative values. For example, the left-hand navigation is set to a fixed pixel width while the main content section varies as the window is resized.

Creating Tables

Tables are made up from the <table>...</table> tag with rows inside <tr>...</tr>. Inside each row are the table cells <td>...</td> marked td for table data. These are where the content – either text or graphics – goes. There are no column tags; the number of columns is measured by the number of <td> tags within each row.

To avoid a rigid block design, you can stretch cells so that they span a number of rows or columns. Spanning is controlled by the 'rowspan' and 'colspan' attributes. For example, in a two-column table, you could stretch the top row of cells across one column to create space for a heading (e.g. <td colspan="2">Heading</td>).

Manipulating Tables

Aside from using the table to format the page, there are attributes which also let you format the appearance of the table. Elements you control at the table level (that is, with the <table> tag) are the width and height of the table, the spacing between cells ('cellspacing' attribute), the padding within cells ('cellpadding' attribute), the border thickness ('border') and background colour ('bgcolor'). While you are constructing the table, it is easiest to set the border to 1 so it is visible. At the cell level, you can alter the width and height of cells, the background colour and the alignment of objects it contains.

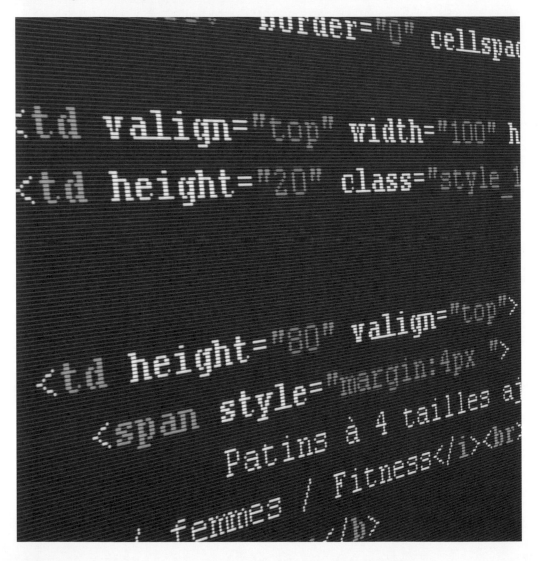

NAVIGATION

Site users need navigation tools to show them where they are, where they can go and how they can find their way back. Just as anyone circumnavigating the globe needs directions, navigation on a website provides the signposts to help you find your way around. It may be the site map, which gives an overview of all that is available, or it may be the navigation bar, buttons and other links.

Structure and Organization

How we navigate the information available on a site will depend in part on how it is structured and organized (that is, its information design). This requires identifying the content available and giving it a shape. That can be a traditional hierarchical structure (*see* page 68), starting with the homepage, where there is a choice of sections, from which in turn you can select further subsections, and so on. It could also be linear, such as a company history where pages are viewed in a set order.

Above: Drop–down menus keep navigation simple while saving screen space

Signposting

One of the complications of the Web is that not all users start at the same place. If they are clicking a link from another site or a search engine, they can enter your site at any point and not just the homepage. Consequently, every page needs to clearly identify the site and have the navigational elements to take users around the site. These elements should look like navigational tools, i.e. buttons should be labelled clearly to show what they are (Home, Products, Shop, etc). It is also a good idea to link to the homepage from every page on your site.

Navigational Aids

Similarly, there may be some pages that you will want to be able to access from anywhere – such as the search box, a help file, a mailto: link, etc. Usually, these will form part of the navigation bar. The nav bar will typically be at the top of the page and is often set in a frame so it is always available. It may also be along the side or bottom of a page.

Instead of a nav bar, some sites use navigational tabs for each section, but these can get very cluttered for big sites (e.g. amazon.com). If there are a large number of links to fit into a nav bar, then a drop-down menu or a flyout menu save on screen space.

PAGE LOADING TIME

This is download time. Even though most of us access the Web at work or home via broadband, there is no excuse for cramming your pages with bandwidth-heavy features such as high-resolution graphics, Flash files or applets. Today's Web-savvy visitors will not wait patiently for images to load, and the secret to minimizing page download time is controlling graphics. That does not mean avoiding them altogether, but carefully preparing them in the right format and using HTML controls to speed up their download.

Limiting Image Downloads

Firstly, images are cached, so, once downloaded, they can be used again with little overhead.

This can be useful for constructing navigation aids where just one element changes between pages. Reducing the number of colours in an image can also significantly reduce file size. You can also speed up download time making sure your images are in the right format – GIF for flat colour images and JPEG for photographs. Make sure that the HTML code contains the height and width of the image together with alternative text. That way, users can check out whether they want to wait for the image to download or click on a link to another page.

Similarly, you can save user time (and patience) by using interlaced GIFs or progressive JPEGs, where a rough version of the picture appears before it is fully downloaded. In the same way, a fast-loading low-resolution version of a graphic can be used as a placeholder, while the higher resolution image loads.

TEXT MATTERS

Most people get carried away with making their website look good – animated images, lots of smart colours, clever links... But, if your text is poorly written and badly placed, your viewers will not hang around on your site for long.

CONTENT

There is such a mass of information on the Web that most people simply scan until they find something they want to investigate further; reading from the screen is slower than from the page – up to 25 per cent slower, according to studies by usability expert Jakob Nielsen. For this reason, it is important to have clear headlines and introductory paragraphs to draw readers in. There are ways to maximize the impact of this 'microcontent', as it is also called. First, keep it short: the headline should sum up what follows rather than be a clever pun – content should not tease the reader; if they go for it and download something they did not really want to read, it destroys all trust for the future.

Write Smart

Similarly, the text itself should be sharp and concise. Generally, readers do not like to scroll, so it is advisable to keep pages down to about 400–500 words. Copy should also be broken into digestible chunks of information in much the same way as a tabloid newspaper does. Important elements can be emphasized by being put in a separate bullet-pointed list or set in a sidebar. An eye-catching phrase can be picked out in a Quotebox.

Text Hierarchy

Content should also be structured – or weighted – by its importance. The main news story should have more space than the date of the next board meeting. Readers should be able to see at a glance the main items.

Hypertext

There are specific web devices to catch the readers' interest, in particular, hypertext links, which are fundamental to the Web's philosophy of interconnection. Hyperlinks can help break content into logical elements. For example, one page can give an overview of a topic, or deal with just one particular aspect. For more detailed information, or an article on a related issue, or previous stories on the same subject, the readers can follow the hypertext links. As links are typically blue and underlined, they also provide a visual 'chain' that encourages readers to scan down the page. A similar emphasis can be used by applying colour to keywords or phrases. However, these should be a different colour to the hyperlinks so the two do not get confused. There is nothing more irritating to the reader than clicking on what they think is a link, only to discover it goes nowhere.

Above: The BBC website provides hypertext links to related stories

FORMATTING TEXT USING HTML

For the most basic formatting, you can break up your copy and add white space. The paragraph tag <p>...</p> adds additional space when it breaks the line. To change the flow of text without adding the extra space, use the line-break tag <br>.

The typeface, colour and size can be controlled with the <font> tag to create a style for the content. The size is not an absolute pixel value, but is relative to the default font size. The size values are from 7 (the largest) to 1 (the smallest). Each step in size is about 20 per cent different. So, if using <font size="4">...</font>, it is roughly 20 per cent larger than the default text size, which is usually size 3. It is also possible to set values relative to the default size 3 by using a plus or minus sign. However, as the browser will not show anything bigger than size 7, the maximum relative value is +4 (that is, the default 3 + 4).

Above: Formatting text using HTML

Size and Typeface

You can change the default font size by using the <basefont> tag. If you place this in the head of the document, it will affect all the text. If you place it in the body of the copy, only text after it will be altered.

Similarly, through the <font> tag, you can specify the typeface, or range of typefaces (<font face="fontname">...</font>, or the colour <font color="colorname or hexadecimal number>...</font>. However, the <font> tag is being phased out in favour of using CSS. Although not fully supported by older browsers, they have the advantage that a single change in style can be applied across the site, whereas, with the <font> tag, it needs to be changed in each place it is used.

Inline Styles

Inline styles are put in the flow of the text to add emphasis, without affecting spacing in the way block element tags such as paragraph breaks do. Inline styles can italicize text <i>...</i>; embolden it ...; or add an underline <u>...</u>.

For greater visual emphasis, text headings can be given different sizes. There are six available, <h1> being the biggest and <h6> the smallest. As <h4> is equivalent to the size of the body text, the main ones used are <h2> and <h3>.

LISTS

Just as in any letter or document, it can be clearer to structure information on your web page in a list. There are basically three types of list that can be defined within HTML: ordered lists (also called numbered lists); unordered (bulleted) lists; and definition lists (which itemize terms and their definitions).

Ordered Lists

An ordered list is good for a recipe, where the sequence of items is important. A number is automatically inserted before each item. Equally usefully, the list will be automatically renumbered if you delete or insert an item. An ordered list is shown by the container tag <ol>...</ol> with <li> and the optional closing tag </li> for each item. You can also change the style of numbering to letters or roman numerals using the 'type' attribute.

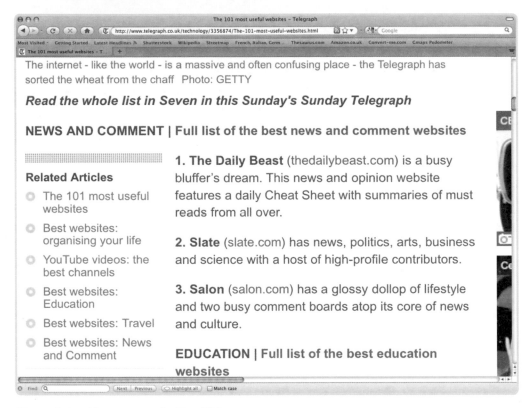

Above: Ordered lists are great for 'Top 10' lists

Unordered Lists

It can be easier to read a list of items if they are separated as bullet points. Using the <ul>...</ul> container tag for unordered lists, the bullets are added automatically for each list item, each marked with the <li> tag.

You can change the bullet type using the 'type' attribute from the default black dot <ul type="disc"> to a circle <ul type="circle"> or a square <ul type="square">. However, these can be a bit plain. You might want to jazz these up with your own bulleted lists – such as an anchor or a smiley face. To do so, you do not use the list tags, as these would automatically insert the default bullets. First, create your graphic, which is usually best saved as a GIF. To make sure the bullet flows with the text without forcing extra space, keep the height to 10 or 12 pixels. For a short list, separate the entries with line or paragraph breaks. To create an indent, add space to the left and right of the graphic using the 'hspace' attribute (see page 103). For longer entries, it is more accurate to use a table to control the alignment of the bullets with the text.

Definition Lists

With definition lists, items are displayed followed by blocks of descriptive text, dictionary style. Consequently, they are also known as dictionary lists. They are marked with the container tag <dl>...</dl>, while each term is marked by the <dt> tag (dictionary term) followed by <dd> for dictionary definition. One type of list can also be nested within any other list.

SPECIAL TEXT CHARACTERS

Not all characters have keyboard equivalents, so they need to be inserted into the text by their special name or number. The ASCII characters used on web pages have the letters and numbers needed, but only a few basic symbols; there needs to be a special way to show special characters, such as a trademark symbol or copyright mark. This is done in HTML by using a special name or specific number. For example, to mark the copyright on your web page, there is no keyboard equivalent. To insert the symbol © you need to put © in the code, or the equivalent number, which is ©. However, the one you are likely to use most is the text string that marks a non-breaking space. This gets round the fact that browsers ignore any extra character spaces in HTML documents. When you do want to add a character space, insert   or the number   in the code. There are a host of other special characters you can use, ranging from the symbol for the pound (£ – £) to the euro (€ – €) and the Yen (¥ – ¥). Note that some characters, such as curly quotes (left – &147; and

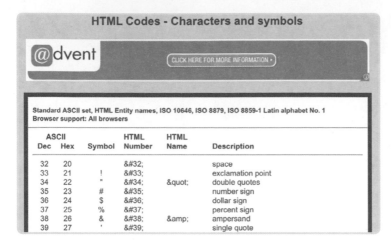

Left: A useful list of character codes at www.ascii.cl/htmlcodes.htm

right – &148;) do not have a name you can use; they are always specified by giving their number. You can find a useful list of special character codes at http://www.ascii.cl/htmlcodes.htm.

ALIGNMENT

In print layout, programs such as Microsoft Word or InDesign let you put text and images where you want, with pixel precision. On the Web, it is a much more tortuous process, in part because little on a web page is fixed. There are a number of alignment tags used within HTML. For basic text, line breaks <br> will wrap text to the next line. If you want to add extra space, use the paragraph break instead <p>. To align text next to an image, use the <img> tag with the 'align' attribute. The text can be aligned to the top, middle, bottom, left or right of the image. If you want to put more space between the text and graphic, use the 'hspace' and 'vspace' attributes (*see* pages 103 and 117).

For better control of alignment, however, it is best to use tables; the same HTML tags work within the individual cells of the table but, by using tables to create a design grid, it is possible to achieve much more. For the best control of all, cascading style sheets offer pixel-perfect alignment.

COLOUR ISSUES

The personality of a site is reflected by its use of colour, which need not be totally constrained by the technical limitations of the Web. Colour on the Web is very different to printed colour because, ultimately, the pages will be viewed on screen in RGB mode.

COLOUR KNOW-HOW

The colours on a page are affected by the browser and platform on which they are viewed. There are ways to compensate for this, such as by using a web-safe palette; this is a selection of 216 colours that are common to all browsers and operating systems. The problem with these is that they are not very exciting or attractive.

However, some graphics programs, such as Adobe's Fireworks, will convert any colour within an image to the nearest web-safe colour. Other programs such as Photoshop have a Dither box, where you can create your own hybrid web-safe colour by combining several web-safe colours together.

Trial and Error

Ultimately, it is the colour of the site that provides the personality. It is often a process of trial and error to get the right balance between a colourful site and one that looks like a paint-mixer's worktop. Using a limited range of colours can make the pages look stunning and well organized. It does not exclude using pictures or the odd extra colour for special emphasis. Colours can be high contrast, or similar, but keeping them consistent on the site makes it easier for users to navigate.

BACKGROUND COLOUR

Solid colour backgrounds can be used with graphic images to set the tone while the rest of the page downloads. By default, a web page is fairly colourless – plain white or grey. Yet it is a simple matter to add some colour. To put a solid colour in the background of the page, we use the <body> tag. This is the tag that determines what we see in the visible part of a web document. With the 'bgcolor' attribute, you can add a splash of interest to the background, but be careful which colours you choose. For example, <body bgcolor="dodgerblue"> might brighten up the day, but it might also clash with the text and graphics you have used. A paler background is 'aliceblue'. You can specify colours by their names or hexadecimal values, but be warned that they will not always look the same to your users as they do to you. The colours they see will depend on how their monitor is set up – the number of colours it can display and the brightness.

The 'bgcolor' attribute can also be used in tandem with the 'background' attribute, which is used to add a graphic as a background image. By making the background colour the same as the main colour in the graphic, the page will load the main colour immediately while the rest of the graphic is downloading.

GRADIENTS

Rather than have a solid block of colour as a background to a web page or graphic, it can be more effective to have one colour fade into another. This is called a gradient, or occasionally referred to as blends.

Blending Colours

Most graphics editors work in a similar way. They have the colour chart or thumbnails from which you can select the colours to blend, and a number of gradient designs. These designs can be rotated by changing the angle value. For a simple two-colour gradient, you choose the initial colour and the end colour. You can also set the transparency of the individual colours. This is not possible in some graphics editors where there are more than two colours. Changing the transparency value affects the opacity of the whole gradient rather than the individual colours.

What to Look Out For

Be aware that, while gradients look fine on monitors set to display 16-bit colour (tens of thousands of colours) or higher, they will appear a bit dotty (speckled) at 8-bit (256 colours). It is worse with certain colours, so set your own monitor to 8-bit colour to see how it will look. Also, bear in mind that gradients increase the number of colours in an image and therefore will increase the file size.

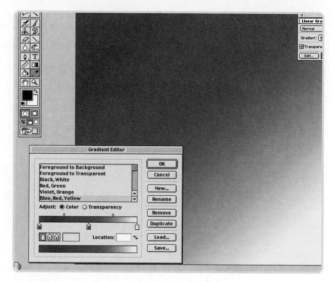

Above: A 16–bit colour gradient

CMYK CONVERSION

Colour format conversion; graphics programs allow you to specify how the RGB colours seen on the monitor are converted to CMYK for high-end printing.

Images for the Web are saved in RGB (Red, Green and Blue) mode, the same system used by the monitor for displaying colours. But while it is the standard way to view on-screen images, if you are intending to use the same graphic for a printed brochure or other publication, it needs to be converted to CMYK. This is the standard file mode for high-end printing, also known as four-colour printing.

Colour Profiles

Each image is split into its four constituent colours – Cyan, Magenta, Yellow and blacK. In fact, mixing cyan, magenta and black together will produce black, but the addition of a separate black ink gives richer tones and deeper colours. In publishing, it has always been difficult to reconcile the colours seen on screen in RGB mode with those printed in CMYK mode. Most graphics programs do allow you to convert RGB images to CMYK for printing. For example, in Photoshop, you can create your own profile – or preferences – which determine how images are converted. In the profile, you can adjust how black ink is used, how greys are handled and alter the lightness or darkness of tone before separating the graphic into its CMYK elements.

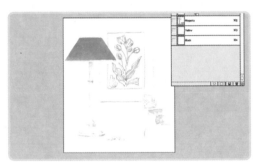

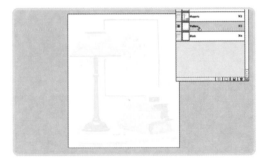

Above: A CMYK image split into its constituent parts (from left to right, top to bottom): the original composite image, cyan, magenta, yellow and black

IMAGE ISSUES

Playing around with images is one of the best parts of website design, but it is important to make sure you know what you are doing. Getting pictures in the right format and the right size is something all web designers must master as a first step.

RESIZING IMAGES

The smaller an image, the fewer the pixels and the quicker it will download. This advantage comes at a price, though: the fewer the pixels, the less detail shown in the picture. Trying to get the balance right, between an interesting graphic and a file size that is small enough to be downloaded in a reasonable time, is a constant battle for the designer.

Image Software

Some software programs help take the strain. In Adobe Fireworks, for example, you can specify the ideal file size for an image, and the program creates the best possible graphic, automatically selecting the most suitable file format. More typically, however, it is the designer who will be resizing the image. There are basically two ways to resize an image: by changing the resolution, which alters the number of pixels per inch; or by adding to or reducing the total number of pixels. Normally, you can resize the image by selecting a new measurement in pixels, by specifying a percentage increase or decrease from the original, or by entering the actual/print size, which also enables you to alter the resolution.

Simply altering the resolution without resampling the image does not lose any data. The same data is used so that either fewer or more pixels fit into a given space.

Downsampling

If you downsample an image, i.e. take away pixels to make the image smaller, then quality will be affected because you are losing data to resize the image. This is particularly obvious if you drastically resize a graphic, from a postcard-sized image to a thumbnail, for example. The image will become very blurred. If you do have to do it, it is best to do it in a number of steps, checking the quality at each stage.

Enlarging Images

If you are resampling the picture to make it bigger, quality is also affected because you are adding pixels. Different techniques are used to try to match these to the original picture, but with varying success. Generally, it is advisable not to upsize low-resolution images. However you alter the size of the image, the quality can be improved by using the Sharpen filter after resizing.

The resize command in most picture editors is different to changing the canvas size. Canvas size alters the dimensions of an image by adding or taking away pixels around the edges of an image, while the resize command pushes the whole image into a larger or smaller area.

CROPPING IMAGES

An easy but sometimes overlooked way to keep file size down is to crop the image. Although most users now connect to the Web through high-speed broadband, large graphics are a real turn-off.

Cropping Methods

A great deal of space can be saved by cropping out any extra white space, particularly with scanned images. Cutting out the background also helps to focus attention on the main element of the graphic. Cropping a bitmap image works in much the same way in most photo editors. Select the crop tool and click and drag to outline the area you want to keep. If you do not get the area right first time, do not worry, simply adjust the crop handles on the box until it encloses exactly the bit you want. When you are happy that the cropping area is in the right place, simply double click inside its borders.

If you go too far and your postcard ends up postage-stamp size, most photo editing programs will let you undo the last step and usually several steps before that. Even so, it is worth working on a copy of the original image so that nothing is lost for ever.

BACKGROUND IMAGES

Using a background image can add a lot of interest to a page for relatively little overhead. A background graphic can fill the browser screen without taking up all the bandwidth, although it will load more slowly than one with just a solid background colour. The reason for this is that the image does not need to be the size of the space it will eventually fill. The graphic file (or tile) which is downloaded is automatically repeated by the browser to fill the page.

Choosing a Background Image

Images can be any web graphic as long as it is correctly formatted – whether a picture, a textured pattern or a piece of clip art. However, while textured backgrounds are good because they add a bit of depth to your web page, remember that they can make the text very difficult to read if they are too obtrusive. Watermark backgrounds work slightly differently in that the image does not move when you scroll the page. When using an image as a background, it is also worth specifying a background colour. This way, the colour appears before the image has downloaded. It also provides a background if users have turned off image viewing in their browsers.

THUMBNAILS

These small versions of images, often linked to a larger or full-size version of the same image, can be used to speed up download time and ease navigation around a website.

Thumbnails are particularly useful for online catalogues or galleries where visitors can browse the 'thumbnail-sized' versions of the product or graphic. When they see one that interests them, they can click on it and are taken to another page where a larger version of the same image is downloaded.

Sizing Thumbnails

By keeping the thumbnails to a reasonable size – both in dimensions and file size – the download time of the 'gallery' page is kept as low as possible. This page should make it clear that users can click on any link to get a larger view. Consequently, it is only those who do who need wait for the larger picture to download.

The page with the full-size view should have the same navigation – or identification – as the rest of the site, with links back to the previous page. It should also have more detailed, or different, information to that available on the gallery page so that visitors feel they have got some added value by following the link.

ANTI-ALIASING

Because everything shown on screen is mapped to square pixels, the edges of curved lines in images and text will have a block effect; an effect sometimes referred to as having the 'jaggies'. In technical terms, images like this are said to be aliased. Many imaging programs, such as Adobe Photoshop, Fireworks and Corel's Paint Shop Pro, enable you to anti-alias low-resolution graphics by blending the edges with tints of the next colour to smooth over the jagged lines. This has the effect of blurring the edges, which, with smaller images, may be worse than the jaggedness itself; it is particularly noticeable with small type.

While anti-aliasing can improve the look of large headings used in graphics, it makes smaller text more difficult to read. As a result, it is generally accepted that type 12 points or under should not be anti-aliased. There are also problems if an anti-aliased graphic with a transparent background is put on a web page that has a different background colour. One way around this problem is to anti-alias the graphic using the colour of the background on to which it will eventually be placed.

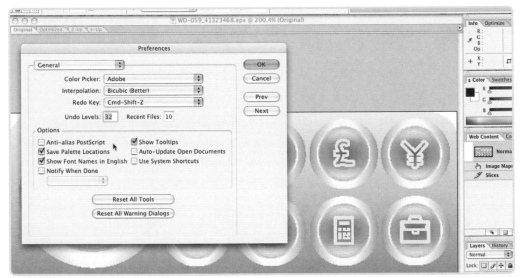

Above: Turning off the anti–alias postscript

TRANSPARENT IMAGES

There are several methods to add transparent areas to web graphics in order to let the background show through and to create more interesting shapes.

One of the best features of GIFs is that they allow part of the image to be transparent. As a result, the background colour or image on a web page can show through and much more interesting design possibilities open up. By removing the typical rectangular box from around the image, you reveal much more fascinating shapes.

Creating Transparent Images

The simplest way to create a transparent image is through index transparency. In most graphics programs, you use the transparency pointer or eyedropper tool to select the specific colour pixel you want to be see-through. Be careful, though, as this is an all-or-nothing approach: all instances of the colour you have selected will turn transparent. So, if you have a red background and a red dot in the centre, the dot will also become transparent. This can be avoided in some web graphics packages by using the Matte colour tool, which is also a useful tool to prevent the 'halo' effect seen on some web graphics, where the edge of the image does not blend into the background, as a result of using anti-aliasing.

Alpha Transparency

Some graphics editors, such as Photoshop, include a much more advanced system for creating transparent areas, called alpha transparency. Under this system, a map of the transparent areas is saved as a separate channel – the alpha channel. The transparency of the pixels can be turned on or off, regardless of what colour they are. This alpha channel is then superimposed over the image to enable the background to show through the transparent areas. It is rather tricky and something for the specialist.

Transparent PNGs, GIFs, JPEGs

The same result can be achieved more simply using the PNG format. This supports variable levels of transparency that enable you to create special effects, such as glows and drop shadows. As with traditional GIFs, the PNG files can also use the simple transparency technique in which one colour is either transparent or not.

JPEGs do not have the transparency features that GIFs or PNGs do, but there is a way to get a similar effect if your web page background is a solid colour. You can create the illusion that the JPEG is on a transparent layer by making the canvas the same colour as the page background before you save it.

Above: Mapping elements of a PNG to transparent

GREYSCALE

For a stylish retro look, it is possible to convert colour photos into greyscale images. It will automatically become an 8-bit image, as the palette contains only 256 shades of grey. It can help reduce file size, and consequently download time, if you are converting it from a file with thousands or millions of colours.

Converting Images to Greyscale

Most graphics programs give you the option to convert a file to greyscale. Alternatively, you can scan the picture in as greyscale. It can also be used to create special effects, such as adding a metallic look to a picture. More importantly, the greyscale function can be used to check on the contrast of pages on your site. A high degree of contrast between text and the background improves the all-round readability of the site.

To check how your pages rate, take a screen grab of your site and open it in a graphics editor, such as PhotoDraw. Choose the Greyscale option and convert the grab. This will show if there is sufficient contrast between the various elements on the page. Do not forget, this is particularly likely to affect colour-blind visitors who have problems distinguishing the contrast between certain colours.

CONVERTING GRAPHIC FORMATS

There are many file formats used for storing information about an image: some are platform-specific and some are program-specific. Generally, though, the main ways images are saved on a computer are as raster (bitmap) files, used in painting programs, and vector files, used by drawing programs.

Saving Images

Vector images create pictures using simple lines and curves that are described by mathematical formulae. Bitmaps use screen pixels to represent the image, rather like tiles in a mosaic. For the Web, images are saved as bitmaps in the GIF or JPEG file formats; a few use the PNG format, but this is not supported by all browsers.

Most drawing programs will be able to save images you created with them as bitmaps as well as vector graphics. However, the compression is handled better if it is opened in a bitmap graphics program and saved there.

Bitmap Editors

Bitmap editors, such as Photoshop and Fireworks, enable you to preview the same image in the three different formats – GIF, JPEG and PNG. At a glance you can compare picture quality, file size and estimated download time, allowing you to alter the degree of compression, the number of colours used and the amount of dither, until you achieve the look you want.

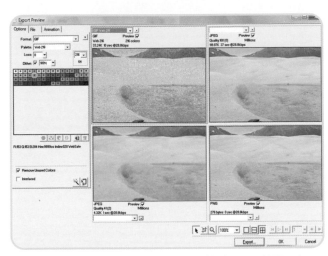

Above: Comparing an image in different file formats (GIF with web-safe palette, JPEGs with quality 100 and 41, and PNG)

SCANNING IMAGES

There are plenty of ways to acquire images. There is an abundance of graphics available on the Web, and the increasing use of digital cameras makes it easy to capture the picture you want. Even so, there are still times when you will have to scan something in – whether it is flat art or a three-dimensional object.

Sizing and Scanning

It is best to roughly size an image you are using to the dimensions it will take up on the web page. Remember that on the Web you need only one image pixel for each screen pixel. So, a graphic that is 200 x 150 pixels will take up roughly a quarter of the screen if the monitor resolution is 800 x 600.

At the end of the day, the final resolution of the image will be 72 dpi. If you do not plan to do any work on the image, then it is easiest just to scan at that resolution. However, if the image needs retouching or changing in some way, it is best to scan it in at a higher resolution – somewhere between 100 and 150 dpi – so you have more pixels to play with. If you scan at much higher resolutions, you can use an image-editing program to remove the extra pixels, but image quality will suffer. If you do need a higher resolution scan for a print version of the same image, it is as well to do two different scans. If your scanner has a menu of fixed resolutions, choose one of those. If you can select your own, go for 144 dpi, which is double the resolution of the final graphic.

Colour and Format

If you are going to work on a black-and-white image, it is better to scan it in greyscale (8-bit mode) rather than as the simple 2-bit black-and-white. This way you get a wider range of tones which can be altered before converting the image back to black-and-white as the final step.

Although the images will eventually be saved as GIFs or JPEGs, it is best to save the scanned files in the TIFF file format, which was originally developed by scanner manufacturers and is very colour-accurate.

CLIP ART

Not all of us are great at drawing, yet even simple graphics such as buttons, icons or backgrounds can really lift the look of a web page. While drawing programs and photo-editing applications aim to make the creative process as simple as possible, there is plenty of ready-made art available online. Clip-art collections offer all sorts of graphics. Most are web-ready, but you may want to import them into a graphics editor to customize the image, such as changing the colours or cropping out part of the picture.

Clip art is handy for providing ready-made navigation icons or for graphics to illustrate links, such as an envelope illustrating an email address. Used sparingly, the images can help break up pages of unappealing text and illustrate abstract ideas.

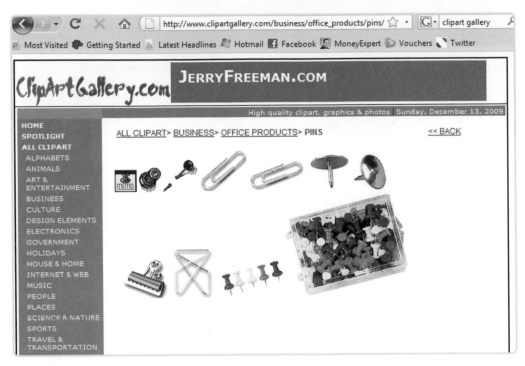

Above: Freeware clip art at www.clipartgallery.com

Sourcing Clip Art

There are a number of freeware clip-art collections (such as the Absolute Web Graphics Archive at www.grsites.com/webgraphics/) or paid-for collections where you can purchase clip art either by the graphic, or by different packages and themes (www.eyewire.com). Most clip-art sites offer other graphics such as decorative fonts for website headlines and royalty-free photographs.

COPYRIGHT IMAGES

As images can easily be downloaded from any web page, there is the temptation to borrow graphics you like for use on your own website. Not only is this illegal, it is also unnecessary, as there are many unrestricted and royalty-free pictures available on the Web. Just be careful, if you have bought a collection of photos that are royalty-free, to check the licensing information carefully as there may be charges for certain types of commercial use. Traditionally, most copyright images are licensed on a 'one time, one project' basis and can attract good royalties.

Watermarks

Because of the potential value of images, and the ease with which they can be copied illegally, designers and photographers are looking to protect the copyright in their images using digital watermarks (see pages 58–59). The watermark can hold all sorts of information, such as who owns the copyright, the audience it is intended for and whether it is royalty-free or restricted in its use.

Digimarc

The Digimarc for Images watermarking solution (www.digimarc.com) also tracks the use of images across the Web. The watermarks are embedded through plug-ins that work with several image-editing programs, including Photoshop and Paint Shop Pro. They can also read the watermark. Additionally, there is an ImageBridge reader, which enables you to read a watermark through the Internet Explorer browser in Windows.

Above: Digimarc's software protects your images' copyright

SAVING IMAGES FROM THE WEB

Sometimes, there may be a striking image on a web page that you want to save to your hard drive – as long as it is not copyright-protected, of course. Downloading such images is best done through the browser, but remember that the technique is slightly different depending on which type of browser you have and the platform on which you are using it.

Step-by-Step Download

Using Internet Explorer, right-click the image (or Ctrl+click if you are on a Mac), select the 'Save picture as' option and select the folder where you want to save it. The right click gives other options if you want to save the picture as a background or email to a friend. If using Firefox, right-click or Ctrl+click the graphic and select 'Save Image As...'.

Similar methods are needed for downloading free images and clip art, although some graphics sites save storage space by compressing the images and saving them as zip files.

Above: Choosing where to save an image after right–clicking

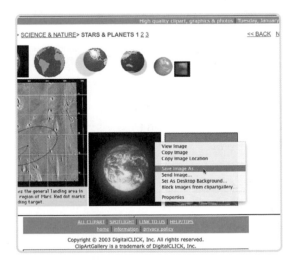

Above: 'Save image as...' on a Mac

SPECIAL EFFECTS

Most graphics editors come with their own set of special effects you can use to spice up your images. In addition, there are third-party plug-ins you can buy to add even more effects. Spicing up your pictures is easy to do with all the graphics programs available today.

SPECIAL EFFECTS PACKAGES

Although each package may vary in the effects that are available, there is a core group common to most programs, whether it is Adobe's Photoshop and Fireworks or Corel's Paint Shop Pro. The effects can be quite subtle, such as a gentle blurring in a picture, or quite dramatic, such as adding a bevel effect to a button to give a 3D look (*see* pages 142–44).

Filters and Plug-ins

While most graphics editors have their own built-in filters to add special effects, some also support third-party plug-ins, such as Alien Skin Software's Eye Candy collection. The plug-in effects can be used in much the same way as those shipped with the program. Generally, you apply the effect to an object and a new set of controls appears that lets you adjust specific elements of that effect. For example, you can apply a glow effect that

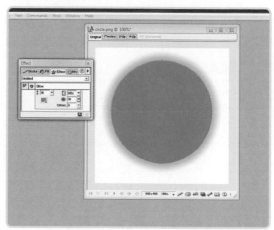

Above: Applying glow effect

adds a colour around the edge of an object. Using the controls, you can set the colour of the glow, its width, its opacity (the degree of transparency it has) and an offset value that enables you to add space between the object and the glow.

Multiple Effects

Nor do you have to stop at one effect. Most graphics editors will let you apply as many effects as you want and alter the order in which they are applied to the image. This can make a big difference. For example, if you create a button and add a bevel effect after a drop shadow, it is a lot flatter than if you apply the bevel effect before adding the drop shadow. As well as bevel, emboss and glow effects, quite subtle or striking effects can be created by applying the blur or sharpen effect. The blur effect softens details in an image by averaging the pixel colours to alter the contrast around the edges. If you choose the Gaussian blur effect, you can control the amount of blur added. Alternatively, if the picture is too soft, or looks a little out of focus, you can apply the sharpening effects to enhance the edges of an image by increasing the contrast.

FILTERS

In photo-editing programs, a filter is an effect that can be added to an image. Some of them are like traditional photographic filters, but many add special effects to the image, such as tiles which break the digitized photo into a series of tiled images. Filters are applied to bitmap images. In drawing programs, such as Illustrator, they can produce the same range of effects on vector graphics.

Effects can be subtle – such as the blur or sharpen filters which can gently retouch a photo – or wild, such as the emboss or wind filters. For that hand-painted touch, try the brush strokes or sketch, while you can add a bit of light to the subject with a lighting-effects filter.

While most photo editors come with a number of standard filters, there are also third-party packages which can be imported into the program and run from the menu bar alongside the other filters.

Applying Filters

Filters can usually be applied either to a whole layer or just a section of it; however, applying the effect to just a section can leave a hard edge between the filtered and non-filtered areas.

Above: Without filter effects

Above: Plastic effect

Above: Coloured pencil effect

Above: Grain effect

To compensate for this, it is best to feather the selected area before applying the filter. In some programs, you can also lessen a filter's overall effect by applying the fade command.

It is also possible to boost a filter's effect. To do so, increase the brightness and contrast values on the layer you have selected, before applying the filter. If you want to make the effect look less artificial, then it is a case of more is better. Apply more than one filter and the effect looks less computer-generated.

Above: 3D effect

Above: Glass effect

Above: Twirl effect

Types of Filter

Effects are generally grouped into sections. For example, in Photoshop, artistic filters such as 'plastic wrap', 'neon glow' or 'coloured pencil' give a more natural, homespun look to images. Blur filters, of which there are several types such as Gaussian blur and 'motion' blur, smooth transitions by averaging the pixels next to hard edges. Brush strokes give that painting effect, while distort filters live up to their name. For example, the 'twirl' gives your image a twister-style effect. Noise filters add or take away speckles of colour, while render filters add that cool 3D shape or cloud pattern to add depth to a view. Become an impressionist with stylize filters, such as 'emboss' or 'tiles', or add a grain or glass effect with a texture filter.

SHADOWS

A shadow effect added to text, a background, photo or button, can give the impression of depth. Most photo editors work in similar ways: select the graphic and apply the shadow effect. Under the controls, you can select the positioning of the shadow (left, right, behind, etc.) and how close the shadow is to its object. You can also change the shadow colour and set its transparency level. There is also a soften control to provide more or less contrast at the edges.

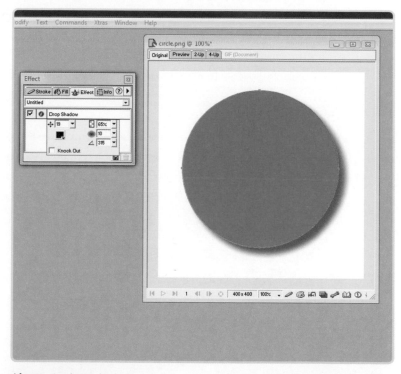

Above: Applying shadow

Applying Shadows

When adding a shadow to blocks of colour, such as a background or sidebar, it is easier to draw a line along the edge of the object and apply the shadow to that rather than to apply it directly. This makes it easier to control the width of the shadow. By increasing or decreasing the line width, you can change the shadow size.

If you save a graphic as a GIF with a transparent background and put it on a coloured or textured background, the shadow looks very hard. The same is true if you apply a drop shadow to text and save it with a transparent background: the edges do not show up at all well. To solve this problem, place the graphic on a white background. If the web page has a coloured or textured background, create a background for the graphic that matches. To do this, create a new layer and fill it with the exact colour or texture of the web page. Ensure all three layers of the graphic are visible – the illustration layer, the shadow layer and the background layer – and export the image as a GIF89a file. While it is possible to do this for most background patterns, it is virtually impossible to match regularly repeated patterns such as stripes.

Shadow Image Formats

Alternatively, with a soft shadow, it may be better to save the graphic as a JPEG rather than a GIF. A softer shadow has a greater number of intermediate colours than a hard-edged shadow and can be achieved more easily in the JPEG format, which supports more colours than a GIF can. The only limitation is that a JPEG will not let you keep part of the graphic transparent.

BEVELLING AND EMBOSSING

Whether you want a ready-made set of 3D-style rollover buttons or a smoothly embossed company name, there are tools to make the process as effortless as possible.

Selecting Bevel Effects

A bevel effect can be used to give a 3D appearance to buttons or letters. Different looks can be created by using an outer bevel (which makes the whole object look raised) or inner (which gives the impression of a raised rim). Having selected the bevel effect, there are a number of options to set. If you choose an outer bevel, you can select the colour of the bevel (if you choose an inner bevel, it takes its colour from the original object). If the bevel appears a bit blocky around curved objects, use the softness control to alter the severity of the edges.

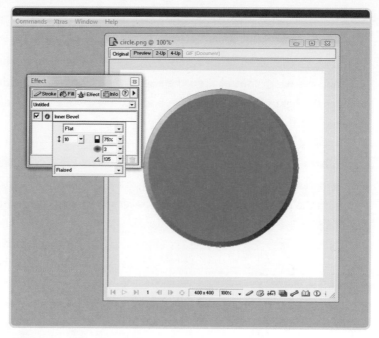

Above: Applying a bevel effect

Applying Bevel Effects

Some graphics editors, such as Adobe's Fireworks, come with a number of preset bevel shapes. The bevel effect can be flat, sloped, smooth, like a frame, or a ring. To change the size of the effect, you alter the pixel size of the bevel.

Fireworks also comes with four button presets to apply special effects to the bevels, which can be handy for setting up rollover buttons. The four states are the default 'raised' button; the 'highlighted' look, which applies a 25 per cent white tint to the object; 'inset', which changes the lighting to invert the 3D effect; and 'inverted', which reverses the lighting and applies a tint to lighten the object. The four different states can be applied to rollovers so that, for example, 'raised' is used for the Up state graphic, 'highlighted' for the Over state and 'inset' for the Down state.

Applying Embossing Effects

The emboss effect pushes the shape of an object out from its background (raised emboss) or down into the object (inset emboss). Again, the effect can be varied using a set of controls. The width control alters the size of the embossed edge; the contrast control changes the light to create highlights and shadows; while the softness control alters the sharpness of the embossed edge.

Remember that most graphics editors will let you apply several effects to the same object, but the order in which you apply them will change the final look of the graphic – as we have seen with the order in which you apply a bevel and a drop shadow (see 'Multiple Effects', page 138).

TEXTURES

A basic background or button can be transformed by adding a texture effect to it. The web page can become a brick wall, stained glass or canvas backdrop. Images on a site can be given a tiled effect or have a grain, paint or glass look added.

Applying Textures

For the background, the texture just needs to be applied to a small image. This is then tiled – repeated – as many times as is needed to fill the background. It is a good way of creating a layered effect as text, graphics and links can go over the top of the tiled background. However, you need to make sure there is sufficient contrast between the textured background and any text or images used on top of it, or the site will be unreadable. You also need to be careful with some textured fills you use that an ugly seam does not appear where the tiles meet.

An alternative to using the textured tiles is to create a false background, i.e. use your graphics editor to create a rectangular image that fills the required space and then add a texturizer special effect to fill the rectangle with the look you want.

CONTRAST

On a web page, contrast helps provide visual clues to what is important. Applying a contrast filter to photos can improve the image. The Web thrives on differences and websites are no exception. For effective design, there needs to be strong contrast on a page, to draw the viewer's eye to what is there. The contrast can be achieved through a variety of effects – bolder text, different typefaces, contrasting colours or rules or emphatic graphics.

The Effects of Contrast

Contrast can provide an important focal point on the page. If everything was the same size, it would seem to have the same importance. By giving major headings a different size, by creating a logo for the company name, by making sure the navigation buttons do not dwarf everything else, you can provide clues as to the relative importance of the material on the page.

More technically, most photo editors have a brightness and contrast filter for enhancing pictures. By modifying these, you alter the highlights, shadows and midtones of an image. Most have a slider control which will boost contrast (i.e. make dark pixels darker and light pixels lighter) when moved one way, or will lessen the contrast when moved the other way.

TILING BACKGROUND IMAGES

Adding a background image to your page can have a very decorative effect – and you only need one tile. The way tiling works is for a single small image ('tile') to be downloaded, which can be repeated infinitely, however big the page. This process is also a good way of creating a layered effect on the Web, as text, graphics and links can go over the top of the tiled background.

Be Aware...

It is important to keep an eye on the contrast between the text and the image underneath. If you have a light background, use dark type, or light type if you have a dark background.

The background tiles should also be consistently dark or light. Otherwise, if you have a mixture, neither the dark nor the light type is going to show up reliably.

Coding Tiling

The code to add a background tile is <body background="tile.gif">. But, like the debutante at the ball, you do need to decide if you want to show the seams. A tile with seams has a wallpaper-style effect. It has an obvious border. To create seamless tiles is a lot trickier, but graphics tools, such as Adobe's ImageReady, do make the process easier.

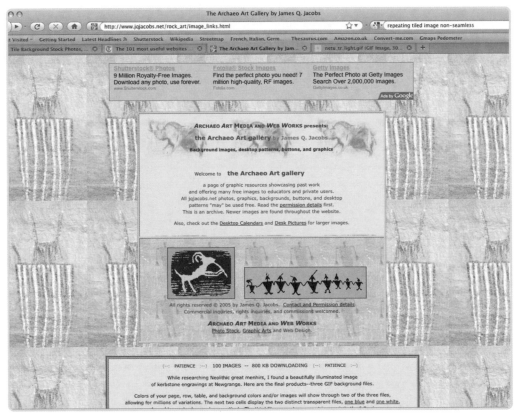

Above: A website showing a tiled background with seams

Above: A seamless tiled background

OVERLAYING IMAGES

Sometimes, you can achieve a dramatic effect by taking the subject from one photo and overlaying the image on to another. Such composite images can disguise your travels. Take a picture of the children in the living room and they can soon be standing in front of Uluru without moving an inch. The key to doing it, using a photo editor such as Adobe's Photoshop, is the 'extract' command. This is a powerful tool that permanently removes pixels, so it is best to work on a copy of the layer you want rather than the original. With the edge highlighter, select the brush size and draw along the edge of the area you want to extract (if smart highlighting is selected, the highlighter will automatically follow the edge as you drag the tool). You can tidy up the extraction with the cleanup tool.

How to Do It

To combine the two images, simply use the 'move' tool to drag and drop the new background on to the extracted image. To arrange the layers, go to the Layers palette and move the imported layer under the extracted layer. You can then use the normal tools to position the images, scale the background or give it a softer look by blurring the image.

ANIMATION

Animation on the Web is becoming increasingly sophisticated, thanks to multimedia tools like Flash and Shockwave. While animated GIFs have been a popular way to add action to a web page, they do not allow any interaction. Another problem with these is that they are bitmaps (in the raster format), where each dot of the image is made up on screen from coloured pixels. A lot of information is needed to describe each pixel in the file, with the result that, if more than a few frames are used, or the animation is used full screen, the file size is excessively large.

Flash Animation

Adobe Flash will give you full-screen, fully interactive streaming animation with sound. This uses a vector instead of raster format, where shapes, objects and colours are described mathematically rather than being mapped to individual pixels. This data is stored in a simple plain text file and it takes relatively little text to describe a full-blown animation. There are a number of advantages to Flash: it is scalable, so images can be resized with no loss of detail; it uses streaming technology, so animations start playing as soon as enough data is downloaded and carry on while the rest of the file is transferred; image quality is high; and it is a good way to add user-triggered sound effects to the Web, as animations can be synchronized with high-quality streaming audio.

Drawbacks to Flash

Flash will also do a lot of the work for you. If you make the first and last 'keyframes', Flash will build all the frames in between and even include actions such as rotating or fading the image. Inevitably, there is one main drawback. Flash files (which have the .swf extension) need to be viewed in your browser through a special plug-in or player, although both are readily available from the Adobe site, and users will usually be prompted to download and install the latest version when they encounter a Flash element on a page. Flash is both a product and an open file format, so you can create elements in other graphics programs – including the whole Adobe suite of packages – and import them into the Flash application for integration into your graphic.

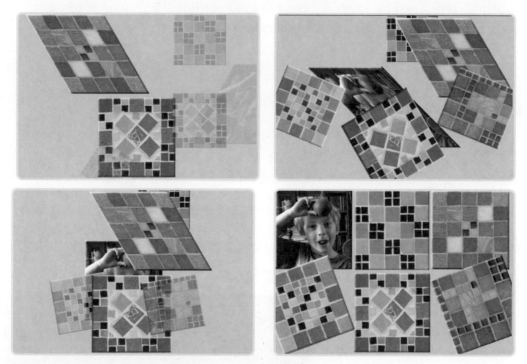

Above: A simple animation using Flash

Shockwave

Adobe's Shockwave is another technology for creating complex interactive presentations to run on the Web. It does so by synchronizing sound, video and animation, which can be imported from other applications. While more sophisticated and versatile than Flash, Shockwave file sizes tend to be much bigger, so tend to be used for more complex applications such as games, interactive brochures and 'kiosk' presentations.

LINKS

Links are the essence of the interconnectivity of the Internet. Within one website, there will be several different kinds of links, including internal, external and those such as mail links. These are key to the interactivity of your website.

TYPES OF LINKS

The main types of links (connections to web pages) are outlined below and in the following sections.

Internal Links

These are the starting points to other pages on the same website and are also known as local or page links. Crucial to linking is the anchor tag <a> which is wrapped around any text or graphic you want linked. To tell the browser which page to link to, add the 'href' attribute with the address, or URL, of the page. This link is usually to a web page, but it could equally be a sound file or a video clip. For internal links, this a relative URL, i.e. the page or file is on the same server as your site. Consequently, you do not need the initial http://, but you do need to direct the browser to the directory where the document is, by giving the pathname. Each directory is separated by a forward slash. If the file is in the same directory, you only need to give the filename.

⊖   **To link from your homepage to a content page stored in the same directory**:
     <a href="products.html"> Product information</a>.

⊖   **To a file in a different directory**: <a href="gliders/accessories.html">Glider
     wheels</a>.

External Links

These take the user to pages on a different website and are sometimes referred to as remote
links. To take advantage of these, you need to provide the full (absolute) URL, including the
initial http://. For example, to link your site through to Amazon.com would be: <a
href="http://www.amazon.co.uk">Amazon</a>.

ANCHORS

In HTML, an anchor is the target of a hypertext link within a document, or a reference to such
a target. They are the tags that form the basis of the links set up between web pages, or to
different sections of the same page. Linking is a two-part process. First, you need to give the
anchor point (the point to which you are jumping) a name and then you make a link to it.

⊖   **To create a target location within a document, the coding is**:
     <a name="name"></a>.

⊖   **To link to that target location from elsewhere in the document, use**:
     <a href="name"></a>.

Crucial

The anchor tag (<a>) is perhaps the most fundamental of all for the Web, as it is the one that
makes linking possible. The start and end tags wrap around the text or graphic you want linked.
Whatever is within the anchor tag shows up as a link in the browser. Conventionally, a linked
text or graphic is shown as blue and underlined, although this styling can be changed.

To tell the browser where to link to the attribute, 'href' (hypertext reference) is added with the URL of the page. Usually, the 'href' points to a web page, but it can also be used to link to images or sound or video files. The URL can be absolute, usually when pointing to a document on the Web, such as <a href=http://www.bbc.co.uk>The BBC</a>. Alternatively, it is a relative URL if it is linked to a page on your own site or server, e.g. <a href="about.html">Information about our company</a>.

You can also use the anchor tag together with the 'name' attribute to create a point on the page which can be linked to or from another spot in the same document. This is useful for finding a specific section on long, scrolling pages, or for getting back to the top of the page with a single click.

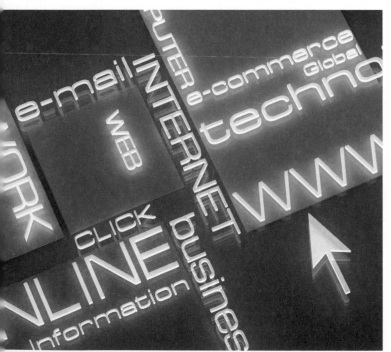

TARGETS

The 'target' attribute is used to specify where linked documents should be displayed. A link with target="_blank" opens a linked document in a new browser window (it does so with any link, not just when set in frames). The default for anchor tags is target="_self", which loads the new document in the same frame or window as the source of the link. As it is the default, it does not need to be specified with the <a> tags. With target="_ top", the linked document will display directly in the browser window.

EMAIL LINKS

While most links are to other web pages or sound and video files, they can also be used to set up mail messages. Instead of the http protocol, the mailto protocol inside the anchor tag automatically opens a new email message, ready to send to a specified address, using the viewer's email client.

However, the browser does have to be configured to use this tag. Most are, but it will not work for all users. One way to ensure that no one misses out is to use the email address as the text for the link. As well as the address of the recipient of the email, you can also automatically add the subject line or names in the cc or bcc field etc. For instance, <a href=mailto:yourname@isp.com?subject="Special%20Offer">Special Offer</a> would write 'Special Offer' in the subject line of an email addressed to Yourname. Note that spaces in the subject lines are written as %20 which is the space character in hexadecimal notation.

Word of Warning

It is as well to bear in mind, however, that putting an email address on a web page is likely to attract spam (unsolicited email) as spammers use automated programs to search for email addresses to add to their lists.

Above: When you hover over a mailto: link, you can usually see the email address in the bottom left-hand corner of your window

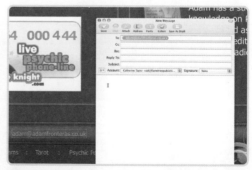

Above: If your browser is configured to do so, clicking on the link will bring up a message window

GRAPHICAL LINKS

Images are for more than decoration. Just like text, they can also be used for links, whether it is a single image, an image map or a thumbnail.

How to Link Graphics

In its simplest form, the easiest way to link a graphic is to highlight it in your web-editing program and select, or write in, the URL of the file you want it linked to. Normally, you can tell that there is a link, or hotspot, in a picture because the mouse pointer changes shape from an arrow to a hand.

Left: Basic icon images can be used as button links

More creatively, a single graphic can have several hotspots – or links – within it. The image is linked to different pages depending on which area of the graphic is clicked. For example, a pet shop website might have a graphic with the different animals it sells. Clicking on one of the hotspots could take you through to a linked page with more information about that particular pet or the foodstuffs that are available.

Image Maps

There are both client-side and server-side image maps. Client-side is speedier for the user, as all the information needed to respond to their click is held within the web page itself. Server-side image maps, although they are slower, are compatible with all browsers, while client-side image maps do not work with some older version browsers.

A client-side image map has three elements: the graphic file itself; the 'usemap' attribute within the <img> tag which identifies which map to use and the map file itself, shown by the <map> tag. Most web-authoring tools will generate the image maps for you. Within the <map> tag there are <area> tags for each hotspot in the image. Each of these area tags identifies the shape of the hotspot, the co-ordinates of the pixels and the URL that they link to.

Faux Image Maps

Rather than having to code a single image map, it can be more efficient for download time to create a 'faux' image map. This is just a composite image made up of individual graphics put right next to each other so that they appear to form one seamless image. The individual images are linked to different pages in the normal way for any graphic. But as individual graphics they can be optimized to produce a smaller file size in total than if they are combined together in one big image.

Web-specific graphics packages such as Adobe Fireworks can make creating image maps or faux image maps easy. Its 'slice' tool splits up large images into smaller graphics, assigns buttons and rollovers to different areas of the image and then exports the graphics and HTML in a package that you can simply import into your website.

One other type of graphical link comes with thumbnail images, which are often linked to full-size versions of the same image. Thumbnails are handy if you have lots of images – such as for a product catalogue – as they download more quickly than the full-size version. Users only have to download the full graphic for products they are particularly interested in.

LAUNCHING NEW BROWSER WINDOWS WITH HTML

Links can be launched in a new pop-up window using HTML, but there are some features, such as its size, that cannot be controlled. Seemingly irremovable advert pop-ups can be extremely irritating, but if you want to link your readers to another site without losing them completely, a pop-up could be the answer. It is simply a second browser window which is opened to display the contents of a link, while the existing page stays on screen.

How to Do It

There are two basic methods to launch a new browser window using HTML. In both cases, you add the 'target' attribute to the anchor tag. Although you cannot alter the size of the new window, it will usually be similar to the one already open.

With the first method, setting the target to '_blank' opens a new window when you click a link. Use this on several links and you will soon have a screen full of open windows. The alternative method is to give the target window a name – such as 'showcase' – which is used as a target for each link. This way, any link that is clicked will open in the same second window (e.g. <a href="http://www.yahoo.com" target="showcase">...</a>).

ENABLE FILE DOWNLOADING FROM A WEBSITE

To enable a file to be downloaded from your site, simply put it in the main directory on your server and create a link to it in the HTML. For instance, to download a whitepaper written in

Word, you would simply have <a href="whitepaper.doc">Download whitepaper here</a>. To reduce download time, compress the files into a single archive using a program such as WinZip. It may be that your browser has a helper application or plug-in which enables the browser to automatically display or play the file. This is possible with some sound and video files, PDF files and Flash or Shockwave files. If it is not possible to play the file directly, a dialogue box pops up, giving the user the option to save the file to their hard drive.

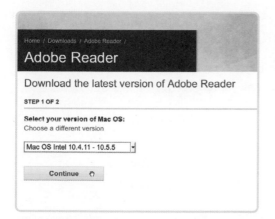
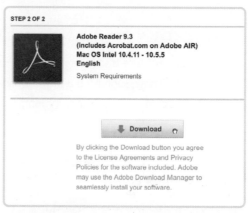
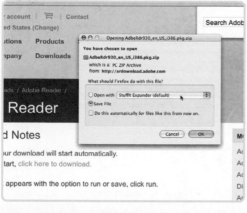

Above: Downloading an application file from the internet

USEFUL PAGES

To get information across – and to aid interactivity and get feedback from your users – there are additional interactive features you can add to your web page. Whether it is setting up a feedback form or posting your CV, make sure you have it all set up right.

CONFIRMATION PAGE

To encourage response from users, it is good practice to set up a confirmation page that loads once they have submitted a form or order. While it is good to give your users a voice, they also like to know that their comments have been heard.

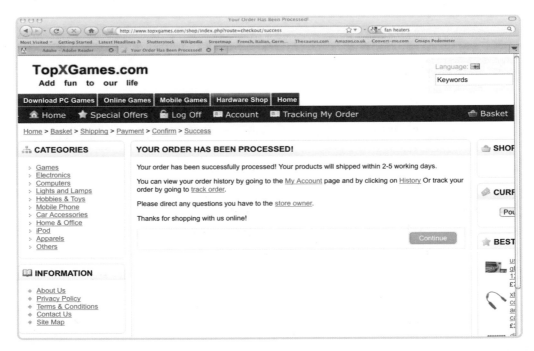

Establish Trust

HTML forms make it easy for users to send feedback or to fill in information for products they want to purchase. But when they submit the form, it is important they get some response that shows them the data was safely sent and that it has been successfully received. For an online store, it is imperative that users get that feedback so they can feel confident in buying over the Internet. But the two-way interaction also enhances the user's experience and creates an element of trust between the two parties.

The easiest response is to create a confirmation page to which users are directed once the form has been submitted. For a feedback form, this could just be a general note of thanks with a link back to the main site. For online purchases, any confirmation page should contain the relevant details of the transaction, including what has been ordered, the amount paid and delivery method. The same confirmation may also be sent by email.

CUSTOMER SERVICE	
Excellent	☐
Good	☐
Average	☐
Poor	☐

CREATING FORMS

It is good to have some form of communication with your website users. The easiest way is the mailto: link, which enables them to send a message, but, sometimes, more structured information is needed. Forms are an ideal way to send feedback or request information.

The form is set up with the <form>...</form> tags. Within the opening tag itself, you need to specify the 'action' attribute (the address of the program that will process the form) and the 'method' attribute (which specifies how the information will be sent). For small forms, use the 'get' method; for more complicated forms, particularly where security is important, use the 'post' method.

Form Coding

For a feedback form, you will probably want a text input field where visitors put specific information, such as their name, as well as a text box where they add general comments. For single-line text, use the <input> tag with the attribute type="text". You can control the length of the visible field by using the 'size' attribute. To limit the number of characters users can enter, add the 'maxlength' attribute.

The <textarea> tag creates a text box for free-flowing comment. The visible size is set with the 'rows' and 'cols' attributes. For example, <textarea name="feedback" rows="4" cols="25">...</textarea> would create a box that would take four lines of text with 25 characters in a line. Any more than that and the box would scroll. If you want to prompt people on details to include, add some text between the opening and closing <textarea> tags.

To round off the form, add a submit button, created by using the <input> tag and putting "submit" as the attribute. Clicking this will send the form information to the URL previously set in the 'action' attribute.

Form Fields

Form fields are the areas on a form where users enter requested information (such as on a feedback form or any other page where a user must fill in information). The most common method will be through a text field, where visitors are prompted to enter details, such as a name or address. Where longer comments are needed, a text-box field can be added. Selection-type form fields such as check boxes, radio buttons and drop-down menus are also used to gather information.

Disabling Form Fields

There may be occasions when you want to disable certain form fields, such as following an earlier selection the user has made. Normally, the browser will grey out these fields so they cannot be accessed. For the selection-type form fields, the 'disabled' attribute will prevent users from choosing them. For text input fields and text boxes, the 'readonly' attribute stops readers from entering any information. However, users can still read the content, so this can be a handy way of presenting licensing agreements or legal disclaimers that you would not want the visitor to change.

Entire fields can be kept from the user's view by setting the <input> type to 'hidden'. These are generally used to help with form processing, where different actions occur depending on the form involved. For instance, if a form is for a new membership, it might have a hidden field marked 'new'. This would be processed differently to a form where membership details are simply being updated, which would have the hidden field set to 'update'.

FORM HANDLING

This is the processing and interpreting data from HTML forms. The best-looking forms are worthless unless you have some way of accessing and manipulating the information that readers send in. Form handlers are separate scripts that take this information and process it. For a simple form, it may be possible to use JavaScript or some other client-side scripting to analyse the form and return the values. Otherwise, the users' responses need to be sent to an email address or to a server-side application, typically CGI or ASP, that can handle them.

Mailto

The simplest form handler is built into HTML. The mailto: form simply takes the information a user enters and sends it to a specified email address. While this is easy to set up, it does have its drawbacks. Many users do not have the interlinked browser and email software that mailto: requires, and the information webmasters receive via mailto: is unprocessed and little more than a string of answers with no questions to guide their analysis.

CGI Scripts

To overcome this problem, Common Gateway Interface (CGI) scripts that handle simple forms are freely available on the Web, and often come as part of a package from an Internet Service Provider (ISP). They can be written in any language – Perl, C, VisualBasic or Java – and all the designer has to do is to reference the CGI script's URL in the opening line of the form and follow the instructions given to specify an email address for delivery of the responses. CGI scripts commonly available online process incoming survey data into charts and graphs, and compile message boards and chat forums. FormMail is the most popular CGI form handler and can be downloaded from http://www.scriptarchive.com/formmail.html.

GUESTBOOKS

One of the easiest ways to interact with your visitors is through a guestbook. Less complex than a fully functional Discussion Board, users to the site simply fill out a form and make their

comments which the guestbook program adds to the existing HTML file. This way, visitors can read the comments from other users. Most guestbook programs put the newest messages on the top. There are a few which operate in reverse.

Above: www.websitetoolbox.com enables you to easily create your own remotely hosted guestbook – such as here – without any knowledge of HTML

External Hosts

Most guestbook programs are CGI scripts, which your server must be capable of running. If it is not, there are some sites that will host your guestbook for you. Rather than write your own script, there are several available on the Web, such as at Matt's Script Archive: http://www.scriptarchive.com/wwboard.html. If you do not have the ability to host the scripts on your own servers, there are many free hosted guestbooks available – check out E-Guestbooks (http://www.e-guestbooks.com/), Anvil Book (http://www.anvilbook.com/) or UltraGuest (http://www.ultraguest.com/).

Guestbook Features

A good guestbook script should have several different features. It should, as a matter of courtesy, send an email thanking each visitor who leaves a message. At the same time, it should send another email to the webmaster or site manager to let them know that a comment has been added. This is partly to save time by not having to constantly check the site, but also enables the content of any new messages to be checked. After all, the guestbook is part of your site's image – you do not want obscenities or advertising plugs to get in the way of genuine messages. Some scripts will filter swear words for you.

CREATING AN ONLINE INVITATION

Some websites allow you to create web-based invitations. These not only allow you to set up the invitation online but also to gather the responses and show the feedback on site. The same system can be used for inviting clients to events or setting up meetings – not just for parties!

Designing Your Invitation

The invitation itself can be as plain or as fancy as you like. Within the body tag, you can insert a background image (using the 'background' attribute) or change the background colour (using the 'bgcolor' attribute). Write out the text of the invitation, with date, time and any special information needed. Use a heading tag to style the main tile, <font face> to specify the typeface, and the 'size' attribute to specify the size of text. Add any images or animations you may have (champagne corks popping, etc.) with the <img> tag. Add some alternative text through the 'alt' attribute for anyone who might have turned off images in the browser.

Getting Feedback

You will also want some feedback from those who you have invited – even if it is just to know they are coming. The replies can be kept separate so only you can access them, or they can be added to the page, so that the other invitees can see who is coming and what they are saying.

To set up this interaction, you need to create a form using the <form>...</form> tags. The information from this form has to be processed. This is almost always done by a program, or script, running on the web server. So, within the opening <form> tag you need to specify the 'action' attribute (which is the address of the program that will process the form) and the 'method' attribute, which specifies how the information will be sent. Typically, this will be by the 'post' method, rather than the 'get' method.

Setting Up Form Feeds

Next, you need to create the input fields on the form itself. This could be a variety of types. For example, if you want to offer several choices from which the invitees can only choose one (such as 'Yes, I am coming' or 'No, I am not coming'), you would use a radio button. If you want them to specify how many friends they want to bring with them, you could have a drop-down list of numbers from which they can select.

Obviously you need to know who is replying, so you will want a text input field where they can put their name or other details you might want (such as a mobile phone number or what fancy dress costume they are planning to wear). To help build up some of the pre-party banter, the <textarea> tag creates a text box for free-flowing comment. You can set the visible size of it using the 'rows' and 'cols' attributes. For example, <textarea name="comments" rows="6" cols="30">...</textarea> would create a box that would take six lines of text with 30 characters in a line. If there is more text, scroll bars appear so that it can be read. If you want to prompt people on any details to include, add your own text between the opening and closing <textarea> tags and it will appear by default.

To finish off, the form needs a submit (or send) button. This is created by using the <input> tag and adding "submit" as the attribute. Clicking this will send the form details for processing by the program at the URL you specified in the 'action' attribute.

Issuing Invitations

Having completed the invitation itself and the feedback form, the complications come in issuing the invitations and processing the data. For simple forms, it is possible to use JavaScript or some other client-side scripting to analyse the form and return the values. But for this type of work it will probably need a server-side application, typically CGI or ASP. For those with no experience of programming, there are a number of online sites where you can download scripts, which can be easily modified by following the instructions given.

Having set up the invitation, you need to make your friends aware of it. To do so, the script needs to send an automatic email to the party guests with a link to the URL where they can view the invite. Once they have seen the invite and responded, that information can either be collated and sent as an email message to you or set out on a web page. Alternatively, in the same way as a guestbook, the comments can be shown on the invitation page for the other guests to see.

External Invitation Sites

All of this may involve some complicated programming. Your server has to support CGI scripts. An alternative is to use some of the online services that will run the whole process for you, such as www.evite.com, the more commercially oriented www.eventlauncher.com or the more specialized

Above: Free online invitations are available via www.evite.com

www.meetingwizard.com. Most online services supply templates for the invitations, but some also allow you to send your own custom-designed invites.

BLOGS

If you are building a personal website simply to express your thoughts and feelings, show a few photos and share your favourite web pages with visitors, consider starting a blog.

Above: Adding new entries to a blog is simply a matter of entering a headline and your text into a simple form and pressing Publish

Blog Origins

Blogs – short for 'weblogs' – have been around since the late 1990s, and the billions that exist today come in many flavours. Some are personal, reflecting someone's general thoughts on the world. Some are subject-specific, following a sports team or a pop group, or perhaps commenting on political issues.

Corporations have also got in on the act, using blogs to communicate with customers in an informal way. Microsoft's Windows 7 team, for instance, shared their progress on the development of the operating system through a series of blog postings, and media companies such as *The Times* or the BBC encourage their writers to publish blogs and invite comments from the public, building a rapport with their readership that closed web pages cannot.

Starting a Blog

Starting a blog requires no HTML knowledge whatsoever. Wordpress.com, Blogger.com and LiveJournal.com are all hosted blogging services, which means all you have to do is sign up, log in, choose your blog name and start writing using a simple forms-based CMS.

Once you get used to that, you can add sections and channels, and even customize colour schemes and designs, and all the systems come with optional modules like polls, image galleries, RSS feed readers and tag clouds – a visual representation of the most popular topics on your blog – which you can activate if desired. Some even let you plug in simple text-based advert servers so you can make a few pennies to fund your hobby, and rather than waiting for people to stumble across your blog, you can add DiggIt or Facebook buttons to make it easy for others to recommend your latest posting on social network sites.

Sideline Blogs

If you want to add a blog as a sideline to a business website, you can download more sophisticated blogging software for free and host and manage it on your own server. This means it will get a more businesslike URL (blog.mybusiness.com rather than mybusiness.blogger.com, for instance) and you will have slightly more control over the appearance of the blog. MovableType (http://www.movabletype.org/) and WordPress.org (http://www.wordpress.org – note, wordpress.com is the hosted service) are the widest used self-hosted blogging systems on the web.

PRESENTING A CV ON THE WEB

As more and more recruitment is done online, it is increasingly important for potential employers to be able to access your CV on the Web. Many designers, whether freelance or employed, have an online portfolio of their work to showcase their skills. Often the About Me page is a CV, highlighting what work experience they have. One of the great advantages of putting your CV on the Web is that it can easily be updated whenever there is something significant to add.

Online CVs can also reflect your personality and style, in ways a standard CV never can. Some CVs are set out like FAQs, listing everything from the designer's favourite drink to their regular bedtime; others are more like web-logs, detailing current passions, while standard CVs concentrate on work-based achievements and skills. This example focuses on putting a traditional CV online.

Planning Content

Before you start, it is best to get the content up to scratch. As it reflects your professionalism, you want something that is smart, snappy and intriguing enough to make employers want to find out more about you. Generally, recruitment consultants advise that your CV should:

➔ **Summarize**: Start with a 30-word summary that sums you up and is your personal 'mission statement'.

➔ **Be simple**: Have a clear and uncluttered layout.

➔ **Be chronological**: That is, set out your employment starting with your current job and working back to previous ones. It should also begin with your employment and go into other details, such as education, technology skills, contact information, etc.

➔ **Be active**: Use active words rather than passive ones, avoid jargon, be concise and be free of spelling and grammatical mistakes.

Columns

Simply putting the text on a web page and uploading it to your site is not going to leave much of an impression. Here, we are going to set up a three-column table to bring some contrast to the layout and to break up the information into easily read chunks. (For the purpose of this exercise, we are assuming that this page is just one of several on the website and will have all the standard navigation features.)

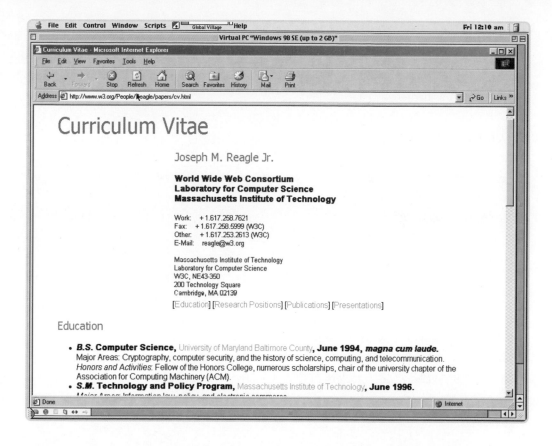

The left-hand column will contain the main CV information, while the right-hand column will hold related information – such as thumbnails of some of the sites worked on or a list of publications where your work has appeared, etc. The middle column uses a spacer GIF to create some white space between the two other columns (acting like a gutter). The spacer GIF gets around the problem that tables adjust their width and height according to the longest object in the row or column, and is a 1 pixel by 1 pixel image which is either transparent or has the same background colour as the table. Using the 'width' attribute, this can then be resized to the dimension you want and will keep the table from collapsing in on itself (e.g. <img src="spacer.gif" width="17" height="1">).

In the left-hand table, we nest a new two-column table, with cellpadding set to 5 so that the text does not go up to the edge of the table. For our 'mission statement' box, we want to span both columns, so use the attribute colspan="2" within the <td> tag. Set out your statement and format the text as desired.

Down to Business

Insert a new table row (<tr>) and table cell with a non-breaking space to create some white space before the main heading e.g.:

```
<tr>
<td colspan="2">&nbs;</td>
</tr>
```

Insert a new row and cell for the heading Experience and change the background colour (using the 'bgcolor' attribute) to give it some impact. Under this heading, we want the left-hand column to show the dates we held a particular job and then the right-hand box to give details of the company and the position we held, e.g.:

```
<tr>
<td width="18%" valign="top" bgcolor="#CCCCCC" class="cvtext">2002-present</td>
<td width="82%" class="cvtext" bgcolor="FFFFCC"> Designer, Bloggs and Co...etc...</td>
</tr>
```

Again, the columns are differentiated by having different background colours, but they are light enough to ensure the text is legible. Here, cascading style sheets are used to apply the text formatting.

Emphasizing Content

There are a number of ways the content can be emphasized, besides the headings themselves. To enable employers to scan read your achievements in each job, it is best to set them out as bullet points. Using the <ul>...</ul> container tag for unordered lists, the bullets are added automatically for each list item, marked with the <li> tag. You can change the default bullet type to a circle <ul type="circle"> or a square <ul type="square"> or you can create your own icons. Company names or the titles of jobs you held can be highlighted in one colour and the URLs of websites you have been involved with can be marked in another.

While this is a fairly simple table design, the possibilities online are virtually endless. You can set up the CV as an image map that takes you to different pages for each section; or include disjointed rollovers, so that highlighting a URL swaps the image on view; or use Flash to create animated timelines.

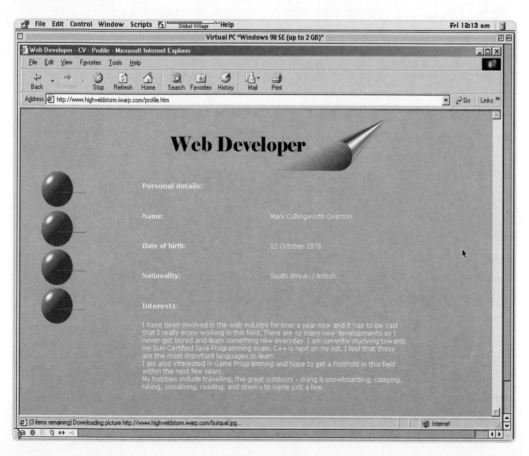

LAUNCHING YOUR WEBSITE

Once your basic website is designed, it's time to get it out there. The first step is a thorough test before launch. Then it's all systems go – upload it and make sure people will come across it when using a search engine.

TESTING

The first area for testing, especially for designers, is the look and feel. Check every page to make sure they are consistent in layout, colour and style. Also check the coding. W3C have an online validation service but most web-authoring tools have built-in HTML checkers. For more advanced proofing, there are special programs such as CSE HTML Validator (www.htmlvalidator.com).

Above: CSE HTML Validator

Validators

Most validators will also perform basic functional checks, such as verifying every link in the site. But beyond testing the structure of the site, it is also important to check it matches its purpose with some form of user testing. This does not necessarily mean a full usability test, but it is worth working through the main tasks likely to be carried out on the site, to ensure they work smoothly and efficiently.

You must also ensure your site will work with different systems and browsers. Most of us cannot keep a bank of computers available for testing, but there are online services such as NetMechanic (www.netmechanic.com) which do and will send a snapshot of your pages taken from different combinations of browser and platform (*see* pages 88–89).

Usability Testing

You should also make time for usability testing. Some companies specialize in this discipline, filming users performing sequences of preset tasks to make sure that a site's navigation and design is optimized as much as possible. Your budget may not stretch to this, but you can still get a few friends or colleagues to look round the site before it goes live. Ask them to find a certain page from the homepage, for instance – if they struggle, something as basic as the wording on your navigation menu could be in need of changing.

UPLOADING A WEBSITE

Once finished, the website has to be published and made available to its audience. This provides the designer with their most regular link to the web server – uploading the finished pages. The standard way to transfer these files (the HTML documents, graphics and other files) between computers on the Internet is by FTP (File Transfer Protocol).

Above: If only it were this simple!

FTP Software

There are a number of programs that make this whole procedure drag-and-drop simple, such as CuteFTP and LapLink FTP for the PC and the aptly named Fetch on the Macintosh. Additionally, FTP functions for uploading and synchronizing the pages are built into many of the web-authoring tools, such as Adobe Dreamweaver.

Whichever tool you use, the process is similar. You first need to connect to the ISP's Web server where your site is being hosted. For security reasons, it is unlikely that your personal web directory will be accessible by anonymous users. So you will also need a username and password to log on to the directory where you will place the HTML pages and any graphics files that go with it. These details, together with the exact name of your server, need to be entered into the FTP program you are using. Once connected, find the directory on the server where you want to copy your files. You may need to create this directory or remove files and folders that are already there.

Plain Text or Binary

Depending on your program, you may need to specify whether the data should be sent as plain text files (ASCII mode) as with HTML documents, or in binary mode, such as the graphics or multimedia files. Some programs will determine this for you and, by selecting the 'auto' option, it is possible to transfer the whole site, including files of both types, in the one session. However, it is not always 100-per-cent reliable.

Instead of the well-understood terms downloading and uploading, most programs will stick to the traditional FTP terminology of 'getting' and 'putting'. The 'put' command uploads files, that is, sends them from your PC to the web server. The 'get' command downloads the pages, so files are transferred from the web server to the PC.

BANNERS

As essential to commercial websites as the ads on television, the banner ad is the original and now the standard online advertising medium. Typically, clicking on a link within the banner ad will launch the advertiser's website in a new page.

Originally, the cost of such ads was based on page impressions (the number of people who could potentially see it) and, while large campaigns are still bought in 1,000-visitor units (cost-per-thousand or CPM), ad sales are now often linked to the number of people who click through to the advertiser's site (called cost-per-click or CPC) or, less frequently, to the number of visitors who click through and buy a product, register for a service or complete a questionnaire (cost-per-action or CPA).

Banner Development

As part of the continuing battle to catch the user's attention, banner ads have gone from plain text and pictures to all-dancing animations and video, and now increasingly complex interactive ads which expand to fill a large part of the page when the user hovers over them. The downside of this is that it is proving increasingly annoying to many users.

Banner Sizes

There are several 'standard' banner-ad sizes, of which the most common is 468 x 60 pixels. Other common sizes are the Skyscraper, a 160 x 600-pixel ad that stands to the right of the page content, and the Leaderboard, a larger 720 x 90-pixel banner that usually sits at the foot of the page.

Advertisers are always keen to be placed in a prominent position – usually as close to the top of the page as possible – while designers are keen to differentiate banner ads from content by adding rules, borders and spaces. One compromise has been the growth of the mid-page unit (MPU), a prominent ad usually around 300 x 250 pixels in size which sits in the centre of the page and has the main text run around it.

SEARCH ENGINES

Although there are hundreds – if not thousands – of search engines on the Web, there are only a few key sites that are used for the majority of searches; these include Google, Yahoo! and Microsoft's Bing. Typing in a keyword or phrase will return a list of sites, along with a brief description, a link and, in some search engines, a rating of how likely it is to match the information requested. If you want your site to be noticed, therefore, it is important you register your site with these search engines.

Most search engines work by sending out a spider that crawls the Web to find as many pages as possible which are then indexed and categorized. Consequently, you can improve the chances of your site being returned on a relevant search by filling in the information in the

Meta Tags. This is used by some search engines for automatic indexing of web pages and for the descriptions alongside the entries.

Above: Google has the lion's share of the search engine market

GOOGLE ANALYTICS

It is helpful to know who is visiting your site, how they are getting there, how long they are staying and where they are from. If you want to increase your readership, this information can help you modify content, site design and navigation to target the most loyal readership.

Some firms spend good money on software that analyses such data, but Google's Analytics does it all for free. Simply open a free Google account at www.google.com/analytics, download a few lines of code and add it to the bottom of every page on your site. Within a few days, you will be able to see how popular your site is, which pages have had the most visitors and even what search terms visitors used to find the site.

Other data it provides includes what browsers, operating systems and resolutions your readers are using, invaluable if you are planning a redesign or thinking about using the latest technologies on your site.

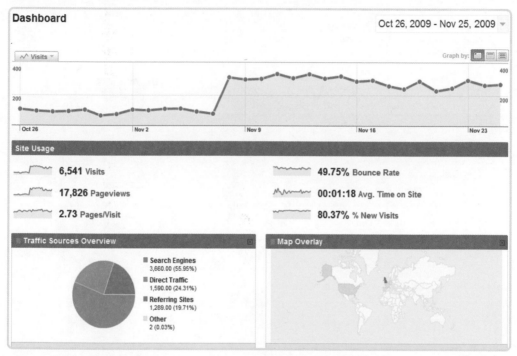

Above: Google Analytics reveals who is visiting your site and more – all for free

GOOGLE CUSTOM SEARCH

If your site is regularly updated and content is starting to get lost away from the front page, you can still keep it live by adding a local search engine to your site. Simply sign up for a free Google account, go to the Custom Search page at www.google.com/cse, click Create a Custom Search Engine and complete the form, adding your site or sites into the 'Sites to search' box. Click Next and the code to add the search box to your site will be emailed to you.

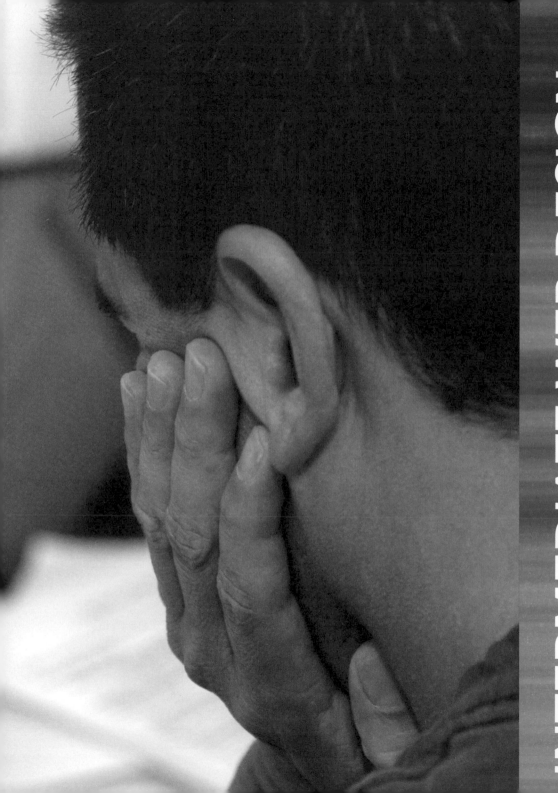

INTERMEDIATE WEB DESIGN

HTML TAGS

Tags are the building blocks of HTML, the most basic elements of any web page. Most developers today use graphical web editors that write the code according to which elements you place on the page and how you edit them. Even so, by understanding the function of each tag, you will be able to tweak the code by hand (hard coding) to correct or fine-tune your pages.

UNDERSTANDING TAGS

Everything from a page's title to the details of a hyperlink and properties of an inline image is contained in a tag. All tags are contained in angled brackets ('<' and '>') and, while some – such as <b> – stand alone, most can be modified by inserting additional attributes within the brackets.

Most tags also require closing. If you italicize a word using <i>, for example, add </i> afterwards or the remainder of your page content will be italicized.

Tags are not case-sensitive, although you should be consistent within documents. Writing them in upper case helps them stand out from the displayed content of the page – but *see* page 101.

```
<html>
 <head>
  <title>Contact us
   <meta http-equi
    <link rel="sho
     <script type=
      <script>
       </head>
        ble clas
```

<HTML></HTML>

The HTML tag is the container for an HTML document, and should form the first and last line of each page. It tells the browser that the data contained within is written in HTML.

<HEAD></HEAD>

The <head> tag gives the browser more information about a page, and typically contains four other tags, <meta>, <style>, <link> and <title>. Details of the page's content (as a reference for search engines), author and the ISO character set are give by the <meta> tag. The <style> tag sets style sheet rules by containing a list of character definitions ending with the closing </style> tag. External cascading style sheet definitions are linked using the <link> tag as follows: <link rel="stylesheet" href="style.css" type="text/css">. The <title> tag contains the legend that appears in the title bar of the browser. Quote the site name and a specific description, as this will appear if the site is bookmarked by a user. Close with the command </title>.

<BODY></BODY>

The <body> tag surrounds the entire visible content of a page, and its attributes define the colour of the document and its text content. While CSS now define text styles more efficiently, you should include 'text' and 'link' attributes for users of older browsers. The 'bgcolor' attribute defines a page's background colour, while 'background' loads and tiles a background image. Other <body> attributes set the size of margins in pixels.

<P>, <BR>, <HR>

Standard HTML has two ways of breaking lines. The paragraph tag <p> inserts a double-line break at the end of each paragraph, while the line-break tag <br> merely turns a line at the point where the tag is added. <p> can carry the 'class' attribute, which defines a style for the whole paragraph according to an attached style sheet. Paragraphs should be closed using </p>. Extra emphasis can be given to a line break by adding a horizontal rule using the <hr> tag. Variables include 'width' (in pixels or per cent) and 'color'.

<B>, <I>, <U>

Basic text formatting tags embolden, italicize and underline text respectively. End formatting with a closing tag, for example, </b>.

<A...></A>

Anchor or hyperlink tag. The 'href' attribute specifies the destination page, while the <target> tag places the linked page into a frame or a new window. You can use the 'name' attribute elsewhere on a page to place an anchor. All the elements between the <a> and </a> tags will become an active hyperlink.

<IMG>

The <img> tag places an inline image into a page. The location of the image is specified by the 'src' attribute. The 'align' attribute specifies the position of the image in relation to the page ('left', 'right', 'center') or in relation to the line of text ('top', 'middle', 'bottom'). The 'vspace' and 'hspace' attributes define the amount of pixels placed around the image, while 'alt' defines text that appears until the image loads completely. 'Height' and 'width' can also be specified, usually to create a placeholder rather than to resize the image, unless a single-pixel spacer is used.

<TABLE><TR><TD></TD></TR></TABLE>

Table tags can be difficult to follow, especially in tabular layouts with nested tables. The <table> tag defines the position of a table and, like an image, uses the 'align' attribute. Its 'border' attribute sets the thickness of the bevelled border, and 'bgcolor' and 'background' properties work as they do for the <body> tag. Additional space can be placed between cells using the 'cellspacing' and 'cellpadding' attributes. Inside each <table> tag, the beginning and end of each row is defined by <tr>, while each cell is contained within <td> tags or, to emphasize the top line of a table, the <th> tags, which apply bold and centred text effects. Cells can be merged using 'rowspan' and 'colspan' properties.

<FONT>

CSS will eventually kill off the <font> tag, but it is still worth supporting for the sake of older systems. Its primary attributes are 'face', 'color' and 'size'. The 'face' attribute lets the designer insert a hierarchy of suitable fonts, for example, "Arial, Helvetica, Sans-Serif" – if a computer does not possess the first named font, the second, then the third, will be used. The 'color' attribute overrides the 'text' attribute of the <body> tag, while 'size' sets the relative size of the font from 1 (smallest) up to 7.

TECHNICAL TRICKS

With the basics mastered, you can develop your website further using some more advanced technical tricks. These can liven up your web pages and make them more interactive with the viewer.

DYNAMIC NAVIGATION

Dynamic navigation, where menu items break out of the static to offer more options or simply to emphasize interactivity, livens up a website, engages the reader and offers a convenient way to make the most of limited screen space.

Rollovers

The simplest form of dynamic navigation device is a rollover: a change of colour or image when a mouse hovers over a button draws the reader's attention to a link. Distance rollovers are even more useful, as the changing remote graphic can give text descriptions of the contents of the destination page.

Drop-downs

Dynamic drop-down menus can be great space-saving devices. If your site is divided into 30 sections, it is impossible to run a horizontal menu across the screen, and impractical to run a lengthy menu down the side of the page. Instead, you can group the sections under a few main menu headings, which, when hovered over or clicked on, call up a menu containing the subsections, just like application menus.

The easiest and cleanest way to do this is through CSS. By using nested list tags, you can add fly-outs to your drop-down menus so third-tier menu items appear on the right of the items on a drop-down menu. It is a great way of simplifying navigation on complex sites without forcing the user to drill down through page after page until they find what they want.

You can download and customize free CSS from a sample site such as http://www.dynamicdrive.com/dynamicindex1/indexb.html, or use the generator at http://purecssmenu.com/ to insert your own menu items, add a colour scheme and choose a style, and press Download to save code which you can then paste into your own site.

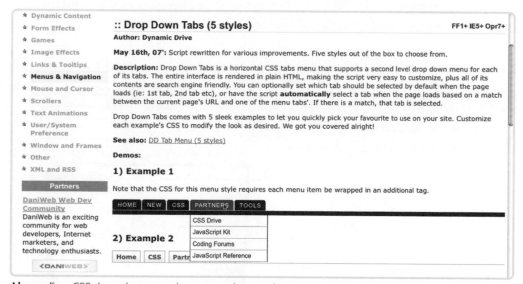

Above: Free CSS drop–down samples at www.dynamicdrive.com

Flash Menus

Flash menus are equally impressive and easy to create, but Flash-less visitors will have no way of navigating your site, and you may still find JavaScript-based menus available to download and adapt to your own needs. With the CSS version so easy to use, complex JavaScript menus aren't necessary, but a combination of CSS and JavaScript can add additional features like time-out, so if a user hovers for too long, the menu will close.

Again, there's a handy generator at http://javascript.internet.com/generators/drop-down-menu.html, or you can download code and customise it yourself from a site like http://spicebrains.com/multi-level-drop-down-menu/

FIXED-WIDTH PAGE DESIGN

When you design a web page, you have no way of predicting the size of the screen and the browser that a reader will be using when they enter your URL. On a large screen, short columns of text can stretch across the page to the point of illegibility, while small graphics can disappear across the wide expanse. On smaller screens, large graphics dominate to the detriment of the words, menus and other page elements.

Screen Resolution

You can reduce the risk of this happening by designing pages to a set width. If you use a resolution above 1024 x 768, you might have noticed that the page content of many professional sites stops about three-quarters of the way across the

screen. This is because the site editors have catered for the lowest common denominator and placed the content of the page within a 960-pixel wide table. On a screen displaying a resolution of 1024 x 768 pixels, the page would fit snugly within the confines of the monitor and, with fixed font sizes through the use of cascading style sheets (CSS), the text and graphics sit exactly where the designer intended.

If you choose a fixed-width design, you first have to choose a width to design to. According to w3schools.com (http://www.w3schools.com/browsers/browsers_display.asp), nine out of 10 Internet users currently use resolutions of 1024 x 768 or more, with only four per cent operating an 800 x 600 screen. With almost 1.8 billion Web users worldwide, four per cent is still a significant figure but, if you want to get more content on to your page, the 1024 x 768 option strikes a good populist balance.

Width Specifications

The fixed width is specified by adding a <table width="XXX"> command after the <body> tag on the page. 'XXX', however, will not represent your chosen screen resolution, as you have to allow for the borders of a web browser's window and its right-hand scrollbar. As a result, the working area of a 1024-pixel wide screen is only 955 pixels, and an 800-pixel wide screen is reduced to just 760.

Because the fixed-width page will end abruptly on larger screens, make sure the design defines the page borders clearly. This can be done by adding a coloured panel on the right-hand side of the fixed-width table, or by heading and footing the page with a colourful full-width logo. This way, the swathe of empty space, which could appear on larger screens, will not look so out of place.

SIMULATING HTML TEXT WITH GRAPHICS

HTML and CSS let web designers specify which fonts appear in their pages. But, while designers can specify several fonts in case the viewer's PC lacks the desired typeface, it is not inconceivable that the reader has none of the fonts, rendering the design process worthless. What can be worse is if fonts and font spacing differ slightly across browsers and operation systems. Photoshop sometimes has problems with irregular spacing (kerning) when mock HTML is produced.

Headlines

However, you can get the fonts you want on your page, regardless of who is reading it, by saving text as graphics – this is really best saved for headlines and small blocks of text. One solution is to create the text to look as you want, then make a screen grab and insert it into the text as a graphic. All graphics packages let you type and shade text, and the best give control over spacing between lines and allow horizontal and vertical scaling. Rather than making a screen grab, simply export a tightly cropped text block as a GIF file and drop it into your page as you would any graphic. Even drop capitals can be added this way.

Manipulating Graphics

When creating headline graphics with a large typeface, turn anti-aliasing on (see page 128) for a smooth appearance, but switch it off if you use smaller fonts, or black type will become grey. Effects such as drop shadows, glows and bevels can be added, and you can fill bold text with a pattern or a graduated tint. Use such effects with caution, though, and stick to your site's colour scheme. And, despite this new-found font freedom, remember the design principle of not mixing too many fonts on a single page – three or four will suffice.

IMAGE MAP

Image maps are inline graphics encoded with hotspots that act as hyperlinks. They are used where a graphical menu aids navigation – a map of the UK could be split into hotspots to display a company's regional offices, for instance – or simply to liven up introductory index pages.

The original image maps were server-side elements, where the browser would have to refer to a CGI script and a separate MAP file before opening the destination URL. Today client image maps are supported by all browsers, giving the designer more control over the mapping process and speeding up page access.

Hotspots

Hotspots can be rectangular or elliptical, or can consist of polygons with any number of sides. Regular shaped hotspots are easy to apply in standard hard-coded HTML. Having added the 'ismap'/'usemap' instruction to the <img> tag, state whether the hotspot is a 'rect', a 'circle' or a 'polygon', and, if it is a rectangle, for example, express the top right-hand corner of a hotspot as x-y co-ordinates relative to the main image, followed by the x-y co-ordinates of the bottom left-hand corner of the hotspot. Add a destination URL and your image map is complete.

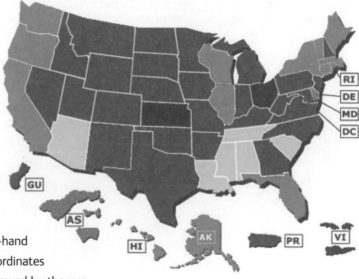

Above: Hotspots can consist of polygons – such as the 'states' on this image map

Calculating Co-ordinates

As you can probably tell, calculating hotspots' co-ordinates down to a precise pixel is difficult, and expressing a polygon hotspot is even harder. Fortunately, there are many tools available that make the job easier by letting you import the image to be mapped, adding the hotspots using conventional drawing tools and creating the accompanying HTML for pasting into the page. Online image mapping utilities include http://www.image-maps.com/, while you can download Mapedit for Windows and Mac from http://www.boutell.com/mapedit/.

Professional web graphics packages such as Fireworks and Photoshop make it even easier, incorporating image maps into entire pages. They will also split a larger image map into a series of smaller images and generate HTML table code to put the sliced elements back together. This serves two useful purposes: firstly, image maps are by their very nature large images, so slicing them into smaller components using a graphics package speeds up loading; secondly, using a web-graphics tool lets you apply JavaScript rollovers to an image map to add an extra dimension of interactivity.

FAVICON

Keen web users will have noticed tiny icons appearing next to site names in the address bars, browser tabs and bookmarks lists in recent years. This 16 x 16-pixel image is known as a Favicon, and is a useful piece of branding as well as an extra flash of colour that catches the visitor's eye.

Creating a Favicon

To create your own Favicon, either design a 16 x 16-pixel image in your graphics

Above: Favicons come in all colours, but all catch the eye on browser tabs or among bookmarks

package, or visit the excellent Favicon.co.uk, upload a square image – your company logo or a photo, perhaps – into its Favicon Generator, click Generate and save the resulting image as 'favicon.ico'. Now upload it to the root directory of your website and add the following lines of code between the <head> tags of each page on your site.

<link rel="shortcut icon" href="http://www.yoursite.com/favicon.ico" type="image/vnd.microsoft.icon" /> <link rel="icon" href="http:// www.yoursite.com/favicon.ico" type="image/vnd.microsoft.icon" />

You will now see your Favicon in all its glory.

Above: Generate your Favicon at www.favicon.co.uk

INTERMEDIATE IMAGE TECHNIQUES

The filters featured in graphic-design applications can be sorted into two groups: non-texturizing effects, which alter the colour of pixels but do not technically 'distort' the image; and texturizing effects, which physically distort groups of pixels to create unusual effects. There are also many ways you can enhance, retouch and so on.

EFFECT AND DISTORTION TECHNIQUES

The most basic non-texturizing effect is to alter the brightness of an image in order to promote or demote it in relation to other elements in the composition. Blending it with a background colour is one option: darken an image on a black background or lighten it on white and you can place almost any image or text element over it, including a fully saturated version of the same image.

Colour Effects

If you wanted to place an image in the background of a montage, but it was proving too bright to allow coloured text to stand out over it, you could reduce its prominence by desaturating it and converting it to greyscale.

Similarly, your graphics package will let you render the image in shades of a colour featured in a site's overall scheme or that complements the colour of the foreground element.

Such effects can be mixed and applied to different parts of an image using masks. Use sparingly, though – desaturating one part of an image and increasing the saturation on another can lead to garish colour clashes.

Texturizing

Most effects are in the texturizing camp. These tools edit selected areas of an image by distorting the order of the pixels. There is an endless stream of such filters and, while some are merely eye candy, a few can be useful when creating montages and illustrations.

Like desaturation, the blur filter merges an image with the background by softening its texture, making the eye think that it is out of focus and therefore further away. The motion blur and wind filters add movement to static objects by adding a trail of smeared pixels to a blur, but their use should imply a natural movement. Motion blur can be applied as a shadow, which also lifts an element above the surface of the screen.

The diffuse, mosaic, noise and sharpen filters are the opposite of blur, as, when used in moderation, they create crisp, sharp images. Use them to sharpen an object at the front of your composition.

Finally, you will also find naturalistic texture filters like slate, metal or wood. These can create interesting effects, but only when applied globally to a completed image rather than selectively.

IMAGE ENHANCEMENT TECHNIQUES

Scanned images or pictures captured with a digital camera will rarely be perfect; whichever automatic settings you apply, slight variations in focus and

Above: Undistorted image

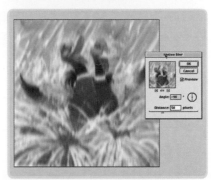

Above: Image with motion blur distortion

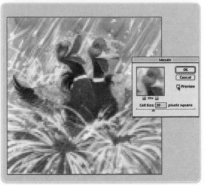

Above: Image with mosaic distortion

lighting can affect the output. Graphics packages offer a range of filters for enhancing such images into sharp, bright, colourful pictures that leap out of a web page.

Brightness and Contrast

The most familiar enhancement tools are the contrast and brightness filters. Increasing the contrast makes light colours lighter and dark colours darker, and such increased definition brings out the detail in most images. It is a good idea to adjust the brightness level as you tweak the contrast.

The danger with using contrast and brightness filters is that the dark and light tones can become too exaggerated, as lightening one area of an image can cause another part of the picture to wash out. The 'levels' tool brings out details without sacrificing definition elsewhere.

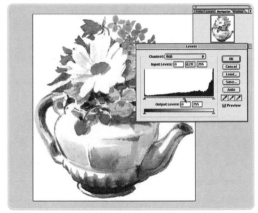

Above: Adjusting the levels

Using Highlights with Care

The colours contained in every image fall into three categories: light (highlights), dark (shadows) and midtones. An ideal image will have an even number of pixels in all three categories. Too many highlights and a picture will look washed out, too much shadow obscures the finer details, while an over-concentration of midtones looks bland. You can alter all three settings but, for subtle enhancement, it is best only to tweak the midtones. Add some depth to a washed-out photo, for instance, by darkening the midtones.

Even after altering the midtones, an image can look washed out if its colour balance is wrong. The Levels tool should let you split the image into red, green and blue composites so you can alter their tonal ranges independently.

Saturation and Hue

Altering the hue and saturation increases the tone and intensity of an image. Every image has a subtle underlying colour, and if it is incorrect – skin tones might have a blue tint, for instance – tweaking the hue can correct it. Saturation refers to the volume of colour in an image. If an image looks cold and colourless, increasing the saturation gives warmth.

Finally, sharpen the image. Scanning and reducing images tends to soften hard edges, but the 'unsharp mask' tool sharpens those areas where colours meet.

RETOUCHING IMAGES

If an entire image requires enhancement, tweaking the brightness, contrast, tone and colour balance can transform its appearance, but such global correction will not clear up blemishes such as dust, hair or cracks, or enliven faded areas. Instead, you can use the selection of tools provided by graphics editing packages to touch up as much, or as little, of the image as you like.

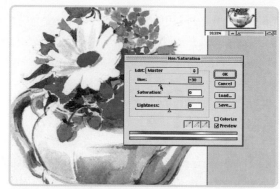

Above: Adjusting hue

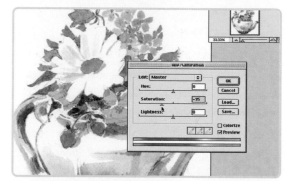

Above: Adjusting saturation

Above: Using the 'unsharp mask' tool

Tool Types

These tools are effectively a combination of distortion filters and brush tools, letting the user edit areas of photos by freehand rather than by applying marquees and masks. Some even share the same names – the blur and sharpen tools, for instance, are fairly self-explanatory, the former blurring the area you paint, the latter increasing the contrast of the selected areas.

You may also come across the smudge tool, which blends pixels as you drag the cursor, simulating the action of dragging a finger through wet paint. Smudge is rarely used for image correction, however, and should be used sparingly even when distorting images.

Light and Dark

Some tools have inherited their names and their actions from traditional darkroom photography, but are easy to understand. Dodge lightens the pixels of the area you paint, burn darkens pixels, while the sponge tool changes the saturation of a selected area. Dodge and burn can be set to edit the highlights, midtones and shadows of a selected part of an image, which will bring out the details if an image is too dark or too light. You can also set the exposure levels of these tools, which, unless you want to create the impression of dramatic overexposure, should always be below 20 per cent. The sponge tool can be set to saturate or desaturate faded or excessively vivid areas of an image.

Fixing Blemishes

Small scratches can be hidden using the blur tool, but larger blemishes might call for the rubber stamp, a cloning tool applied by first clicking on the area you want to copy and then painting where you want the image duplicated. While this tool can be used to create dramatic effects – adding an extra eye to someone's forehead, for instance – it is best used for small areas when retouching, as large sweeps of copied pixels will tend to show up dramatically.

Some photo-specific graphics packages include tools such as red-eye reduction and scratch-removal filters, which are easy to use and can correct common problems quickly and easily.

IMAGE COMPRESSION

Inline images have to be as small as possible, as large images can slow download times for dial-up users and cause bandwidth charges to mount, turning a hobby into an expensive pastime. To reduce file sizes, image compression tools are usually applied when a file is being exported into its web format. Programs such as Fireworks and Photoshop can display the original image alongside a number of previews so that you can try out different degrees of compression on an image and compare the results side-by-side before committing.

Compressing GIFs and PNGs

When compressing images manually, the different formats compress in different ways. GIFs are compressed by a reduction in the number of colours contained in the image. Graphics editors let you specify the palette size, and some let you apply a degree of compression which reduces the colour depth automatically. You can opt to dither colours when saving a GIF, although this can increase image size and reduces image quality, so use carefully.

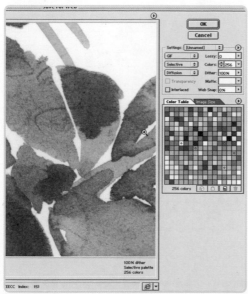

Above: A GIF image using 256 colours

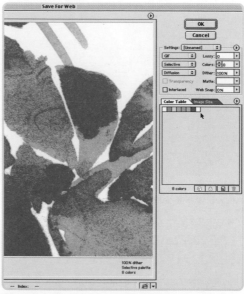

Above: A GIF image using 8 colours

PNGs compress similarly to GIFs, except that they can be saved in 8-, 24- or 32-bit formats. The size of a 32-bit PNG file is probably too big for web use so, if you do use PNGs, stick to 8-bit for low-colour, GIF-style graphics and 24-bit for photographic images. Dithering also has a less detrimental effect on PNGs than on GIFs.

Compressing JPEGs

Graphics editors compress JPEGs by removing pixels that the eye is unlikely to miss. Just how many pixels are combined with their neighbours is determined by the degree of compression the editor applies. This is usually expressed on a sliding scale between 1 and 99, where 99 is almost uncompressed and 1 would be little more than a blur. Every image reacts differently to compression (smoothly graduated areas in particular break up badly), so the export preview should come in useful as you try various points on the scale.

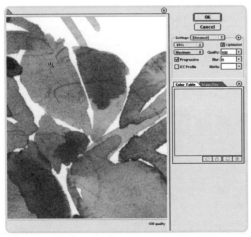

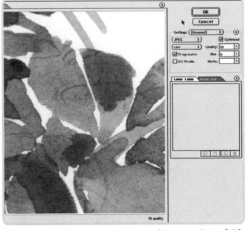

Above: A JPEG image uncompressed (at 100)   **Above**: A JPEG image compressed to a quality of 10

ILLUSTRATIONS

Illustrations cannot take up the same proportion of space on the Web as they can in print but, used properly, they can be both informative and eye-catching.

The Web offers an endless source of illustrations through clip-art galleries and image libraries. Copyright-free images can be combined into montages using Photoshop or Fireworks or, if you cannot find a suitable image, you can edit or create your own in Adobe Illustrator. If you also work in print, artwork could be scanned in for illustrative purposes.

Keep It Simple

Illustrations are best kept simple. Detailed images will not reproduce well when reduced for web use so, if you are using a large print graphic or detailed photograph, crop just one element and use that instead.

Feature illustrations should be used to complement the content, so use sparingly on a page. If you are converting a larger illustration for web use, you could slice it into smaller sections and use a different segment on each page. Choose a bright, engaging section of the image for use as a link on the homepage.

Where to Use Illustrations

Illustrations can be used to encapsulate the spirit and subject matter of a site. On a sparse homepage, a large illustration on the left-hand side can draw the eye and add some colour to the page. Again, the rule is to keep it simple – a close-up image or basic montage with a little creative distortion will act as an eye-catching introduction to your work.

MAKING THE BEST OF BROWSERS

Browsers – software that allows people to search the Web and that display pages – are obviously vital. This section explains how to apply more advanced browser techniques to your pages and how to optimize search engines.

LAUNCHING NEW BROWSER WINDOWS WITH JAVASCRIPT

Gain control over pop-up windows. The target="_new" or target="_blank" attributes in HTML are good for opening secondary, external browser windows, but using JavaScript commands can give more control over the size and appearance of your pop-up window.

Window.open

JavaScript's window.open method is easy to use alongside regular <a href> tags and equally easy to customize. To open a new window, simply add the onClick method to the hyperlink tag as follows: <a href="URL" onClick="window.open('URL', 'window_name', 'window_options'); return false">link_here</a>. The destination URL is included twice. This is because older browsers that do not support onClick will ignore the JavaScript code and interpret the line as a straight hyperlink. Remember to include the full URL (including http://) if you are linking to an external site.

Window_name

The window_name variable gives the pop-up window a name. If you add another pop-up link further down the page, using the same window name would place the new link into the same open window. Changing the window name would open a further pop-up window.

Window_options

The window_options entry is where JavaScript pop-ups really come into their own. Each window has nine variables that can be switched on or off to govern the size and position of the new window and determine which elements of browser furniture are featured in the pop-up. All the variables are switched off by default, but can be added to a window simply by entering the keyword into the window_options variable, separated by commas.

The control options are: toolbar (which displays the row of buttons at the top of a regular browser window), directories (single-click bookmarks), location (address bar), status (the status bar at the

Above: This pop–up window has had all the control options switched on, providing ultimate usability

bottom of the browser window), menu bar, resizable (which determines whether a window can be dragged out) and scrollbars. To specify a window size, add height=xx and width=xx into the window_options area, bearing in mind that the size specified is for the browser's whole interface and not just the page display area. Finally, you can specify where you want the new window to appear on screen with the top=xx and left=xx values. These tell the browser how many pixels from the top and from the left-hand side of the screen the top-left corner of the new window should be positioned.

So, if we wanted a 300 x 300-pixel resizeable window with a toolbar and status bar placed 150 pixels from the top of the screen, then our link would read:
<a href="URL" onClick="window.open('URL', 'window_name', 'resizable,toolbar,status,height=300,width=300,top=150'); return false">link_here</a>.

CLOSING BROWSER WINDOWS WITH JAVASCRIPT
Any browser window can be closed via the File menu or by clicking the exit button (the X in the top right-hand corner on PCs, or the red button in the top left-hand corner on the Mac).

But if your website regularly calls up new pop-up windows, you can make your readers' browsing experience easier by offering a link or a button which they can click to close the new window. This is best done using JavaScript routines.

➔ **To create a simple Close hyperlink, insert the following code:**
```
<a href="javascript:window.close()">Close</a>.
```

Where we have written 'Close', you can write anything – an 'X' in a circle or 'Close' in your house style are good examples. Or even add an image.

➔ **To insert an image, use this code, calling your chosen image 'closeimage.gif':**
```
<a href="javascript:window.close()">
<img border="0" src="closeimage.gif">
</a>
```

➔ **A Close button can add a professional touch to your window:** The 'value' parameter in the following code represents the text that appears in the button:
```
<form>
<input type="button" value="Close" onClick="window.close()">
</form>
```

➔ **An image can also be used for the button instead of the 'Default' button:**
```
<input type="image" alt="xx" src="image-path">
```

SEARCH-ENGINE OPTIMIZATION

Search engine optimization (SEO) is an increasingly important weapon in the armoury of any webmaster. Companies and consultants will charge good money to help push your site up the listings, but even if you can't afford for such services, there are a few tactics you can use to raise your site's profile.

Keywords: The main topic of your site in two or three words. These are picked up by search engines, so make sure you include your keywords frequently and prominently, and do not be afraid to repeat those keywords as often as possible. The most important places to include your keywords include the page title, in headings and headlines, as links, in bold text, in the filename or URL itself and finally in the <meta> tags. Do not however, simply repeat the keyword 20 times and call it a <meta> tag – search engines see through such tactics and may relegate your site down the listings as a result.

Page build: Search engines cannot read some kinds of page and simply ignore others. If you are including keywords in links, do not make them solely accessible through image maps of JavaScript. CSS-based navigation, for instance, is far preferable to a script which the search engine cannot decipher. Very long pages and very short pages are frequently ignored, and pages constructed purely from Flash cannot even be read by search engines.

Inbound links: Try to get other sites to link to yours. Like a fashionable friend, being seen to be associated with a popular site will rub off on you, and your site will move up the search results accordingly.

Google is your friend: There are 200 million websites out there, so the Internet's most popular search engine is not going to find you on its own, is it? Fortunately, Google offers a set of tools that can help you get on the map. First of all, submit your site at www.google.co.uk/addurl/. Then, when your site has grown a little,

Above: Keeping your site map up to date with Google is a quick but invaluable task

sign up for Google's Webmaster Tools and submit a site map. This is a simple file listing all the page titles and their URLs on your site at a given time. A sitemap can be created automatically at XML-Sitemaps.com (http://www.xml-sitemaps.com/) and uploaded to Webmaster Tools at https://www.google.com/webmasters/tools/.

CREATING A PERSONAL WEBSITE

The Web is not all about big business. The majority of the sites on the Internet were created in bedrooms and studies rather than boardrooms and studios, by webmasters who only want to share their hobbies or their thoughts with like-minded web surfers. With inexpensive software and a plethora of online services, creating family pages or a fan site is quick and easy, and can lead to bigger things: a few well-run fan sites have gone on to become the official web presence of some musical artists and sporting associations.

STEP BY STEP

1: Determine the theme of the site and the target readership. If your site is for keeping in touch with far-flung family members, make sure they have Web access first; there is little point in starting work on a site if you are going to be its only reader.

2: If it is a hobbyist or fan site, search for similar existing sites and work out how your site is going to be different and better. If your chosen subject already has an official site, think about how you can offer an informal alternative.

3: Plan the structure of your site, dividing the content into directories and creating a site map or storyboard illustrating each page. Stick to this structure as you build the site.

4: Choose between designing your own site and using an online site builder or CMS. Sites such as MoonFruit (www.moonfruit.com) let you add your content and colour scheme into a standard template. However, their inflexible formats offer few opportunities to stamp your own style on a site.

5: If you are designing the site, choose a web editor. There are several combined web editors/image-editing tools available for under £50, including BestAddress, CoffeeCup for Windows and iWeb and RapidWeaver for the Mac. Adobe's Dreamweaver is a good investment if you see your site as a long-term hobby.

6: Learn a little HTML before starting on the site's design. An editor might not be producing the desired effect and, by understanding some of the code, you might be able to correct it by hand. It also proves useful when viewing (and 'borrowing') the source of a well-designed page to use as the basis of your design. There are many HTML tutorials and primers on the Web.

7: Consider your image sources. Most clip art is of poor quality. Create your own graphics in an inexpensive graphics package such as Paint Shop Pro. Use photos taken with a digital camera or scanned; basic image-editing tools are often bundled with digitizing hardware.

Above: A family website

8: Add value to the site with free tools such as chat forums and online polls. Such features can encourage visitors to return and help build an online community. Guestbooks and hit counters can be the source of invaluable feedback.

9: When the content is ready, choose a host for your pages. This could be your current Internet Service Provider (ISP), as dial-up contracts usually include around 10 Mb of free web space. Check the terms and conditions – there is probably a limit on the amount of data that can be sent from the site each month, beyond which the ISP may charge or press for an upgrade to a business account.

10: If your site is to be mainly text-based and informal, consider using one of the many online blogging services available to host your site. You can customize colour schemes and layout, and the blog content management system (CMS) means you can upload content without having to learn any but the most basic HTML.

11: Rather than using the unwieldy URL supplied by your ISP (usually in the format www.yourname.homepages.hostname.co.uk or sometimes featuring number codes), consider buying a domain name. URLs ending in .co.uk cost as little as £5 a year and are far easier to remember.

12: Choose an FTP (File Transfer Protocol) utility for uploading your website. The better ones cost around £20, but there are plenty of free and shareware ones available. Your ISP will supply the settings for uploading your pages, or an online host may demand that you upload pages using a browser-based online form.

13: Once uploaded, ask related sites for a reciprocal link. Even rival sites usually agree. Find a web ring that concerns your topic and submit your URL. You will have to place a button and some code on your homepage that links to a random related site, but you should see visitor numbers rise in return. Publicizing the site in search engines and directories is also advisable.

14: Make some pocket money by selling products through partnership programmes. Online retailers such as Amazon (www.amazon.co.uk) have schemes whereby you advertise their goods and earn a percentage of every sale in return.

15: Web publishing can be a legal minefield. Do not pass on gossip you have no evidence for and make sure the users of your message board do not overstep the libel mark as you could be liable. Do not use reports or images copied from other sites as the copyright holder is unlikely to accept your amateur status as an excuse not to pay royalties. Some television companies have even banned all fan sites for certain shows, citing 'quality control' as their justification. If in doubt, do not publish – or your hobby could become very costly.

Above: A fan site

MAKING AND MEASURING IMPACT

If you have a business site, your logo is key to your brand – an instantly recognizable theme that should be consistent across your website. Once you have nailed the logo, the rest of the design should follow. This section also shows you how to set up a forum to gauge feedback.

LOGO DESIGN

A site's logo is the first thing most visitors will see on a homepage. As first impressions count, the logo has to be eye-catching, engaging, bold and clear. Most of all, it has to say something positive about the company or person who has created the site. Most modern web logos consist of a graphical motif and the company name. As photographic images are best avoided, the shape should be an abstract representation of what the site is all about. Make the motif natural, as the eye will soon spot irregular dynamics. Any implied movement should be from left to right, and items should appear to rest on an invisible surface – a CD, for instance, should appear to 'sit' on its right-hand side, leaning back to the left. A second ellipse, acting as a shadow, can help emphasize this effect.

Choosing Colours

Colours should be kept simple and realistic. The CD's 'shadow', for instance, should be a darker shade of the colour of the main motif. Choose three or four complementary colours and tie these in with the overall theme of your site. Be natural with colours, too – if your logo is a stylized tree, don't shade it blue unless you have good reason (if the company name is Bluetree, for instance).

Company Name

The final element of your logo should be the company's name. Indeed, this may be the only element if you opt for a stylized name or monogram, in which case, the rules governing shape and colour still apply (the name would stand out more if placed inside an ellipse or square, for instance).

Fonts

Use all upper or all lower case, and choose a font you like from your library. Do not use elaborate script or display fonts as they will lose their clarity once shrunk to button size. Place the name to the right or underneath the motif to conform to natural eye flow.

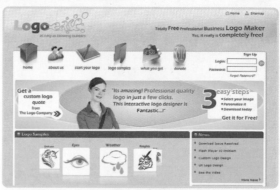

Above: Help designing logos is available online in the form of sites such as www.logoease.com

FORUMS

Guestbooks are a great way to gauge the reaction of visitors to your site but, if your readership grows, you can create more of a community by using fully fledged forum software. Systems like vBulletin and phpBB let you create sub-forums within the main forum, so that visitors can see clearly where to go to discuss specific issues. Users, who usually need to register to write on the bulletin boards, can add their own icons (or 'avatars') next to each post, and moderators have the power to ban users if they need to.

vBulletin (http://www.vbulletin.com/) costs around £150 for a licence, while phpBB (http://www.phpbb.com/) is free to download, although, in either case, your Internet hosting provider will have to support PHP and the associated MySQL database through a Linux server

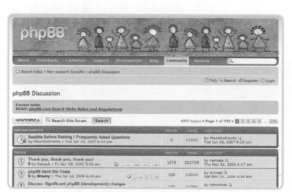

Above: Systems such as phpBB allow you to create flexible forums

package. But watch your bandwidth costs – busy bulletin board software does transfer a lot of information to and from the server, and a successful forum could end up costing you in terms of additional bandwidth charges.

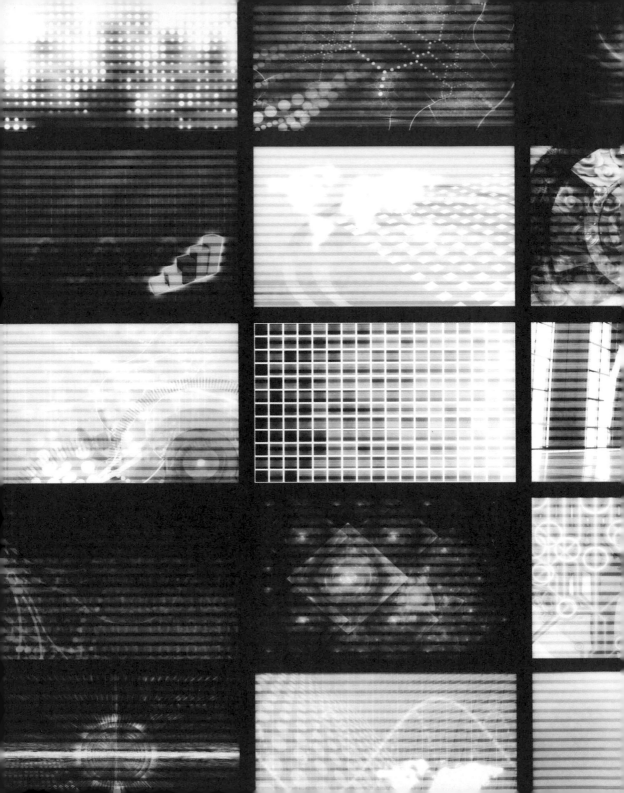

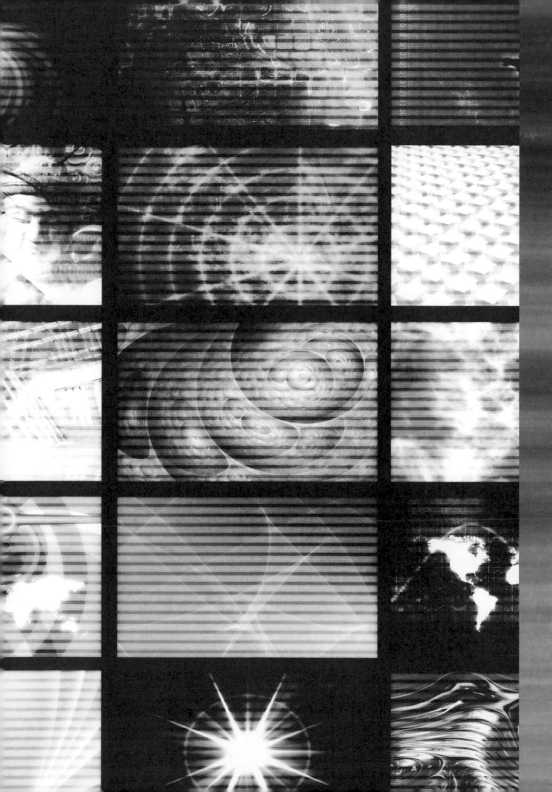

ADVANCED WEB DESIGN

CSS

Cascading Style Sheets give website developers more control over the appearance of web pages than regular HTML offers. The CSS1 and CSS2 specifications, created by the W3C to encourage web-wide uniformity, give complete control over the layout and style of every element on a web page, from text and paragraphs to tables and page margins.

THE JOY OF CSS

As the colour and layout attributes of entire sites can be set from a single remote CSS file, designers can make radical changes to the design of whole sites without having to edit hundreds or thousands of individual HTML pages.

Uses of CSS

Style sheets are even more useful in a corporate environment. With several designers working on pages, being able to define characters through a style sheet is much easier than having to refer to fonts and colour

Left: An example of a website template that is likely to use CSS for ease of styling

codes on every line, where the slightest error could put a page out of kilter with the rest of a site. Likewise, if a head designer wants to make one change (to the size or colour of a site's main body font, for example), all they have to do is change the content of the CSS file.

Simply specifying a style name for each paragraph rather than describing the typeface, size and colour to use at length – a process called 'hard coding' – also reduces the size of HTML files considerably and speeds up page download times.

CREATING AND APPLYING STYLE SHEETS

Using a graphics editing package, designers will find creating and applying style sheets as easy – and remarkably similar– to utilizing style sheets in desktop publishing packages.

Control Over Size, Dimensions and Spacing

In fact, elements such as type size and margin dimensions can be specified in pixels, points and millimetres rather than in the clumsy relative sizes used in HTML. You can also set leading and work spacing, variables that are impossible to change using HTML. CSS1 also sets up items like drop caps automatically, which in HTML you can do only by creating additional graphics.

CSS2 brings further precision with its spacing and positioning commands. Designers can position an element to appear anywhere on the screen and set standard spacing rules for paragraphs and images.

A Little Way to Go

Because measurements are expressed in day-to-day values, the resulting type size will eventually be constant across browsers and operating systems. For the moment, though, the consistency is not quite there, especially with regards to positional settings, and you should check any page designs in as many environments as possible before publishing.

INTERACTIVE FEATURES

Liven up your website and make it truly interactive for your viewers by adding features such as rollovers and iframes.

ROLLOVERS

Browsers highlight text and graphical hyperlinks by changing the cursor from a conventional pointer to a hand symbol but, if you want links and buttons to be absolutely clear to readers, visual triggers are key, and changing the state of a graphical or text hyperlink is simple and effective.

Hovering

Cascading style sheets (CSS) offer an easy way of highlighting text hyperlinks. Each CSS style you create has a property called 'hover', which is activated when the user places a cursor over a link.

Alongside the definition of a style (at the top of an HTML page or in a separate .css file), add a property called A.stylename:hover (where stylename is the name of the style in question). Then specify the character traits you want changed when the cursor hovers. For instance, if you wanted text in the stylename to become red and lose its underline when the cursor appears, add A.stylename:hover {color: red; text-decoration: none} to your style sheet.

While CSS hover-based rollovers are simple to set up, graphical rollovers are far more effective. Although there are Java rollover applets available, these can take a while to load, and small JavaScript can do the same job much more quickly.

Types of Rollover

There are three main types of rollover: button rollovers, where an image changes as the cursor

Kari Goes MacGirlver
MythBusters Raw (02:39)

"The World's Going to Hell."
Mythbusters (01:09)

Badger Bullet Test
Howe and Howe Tech (02:57)

Fish Eyeball Munch
Man vs. Wild (01:18)

Bear's Top Survival Tips
Mar

Duct Tape Hour Outtakes

Above/right: This one–to–many rollover causes a play button to appear as well as an explanation of the video

hovers over it; distance (or disjointed) rollovers, where a remote image changes as you hover over a series of buttons; and one-to-many rollovers, a combination of the two. Button rollovers are the most common, and are usually used for menu items and hyperlinks. Distance and one-to-many rollovers are widely used on homepages, where the user might hover over a menu item and see a written explanation of that section of the site elsewhere on screen.

Graphics Packages

The leading web graphics packages come with utilities to help create rollovers, and Fireworks even has preset bevel effects, changing the edges and shade of your original button so that it looks as though it is physically raised, inset or inverted. All should export the relevant section of HTML and JavaScript as well as the set of graphics required.

JavaScript uses the onMouse controls to change the image and, as onMouse has four states, so you could include four button states. OnMouseOver controls the state of the button when the cursor hovers over it, while OnMouseOut is usually used to revert back to the default button when the cursor moves away. OnMouseDown changes the button state if the mouse is clicked on a button, while onMouseUp specifies the image that remains after the mouse button is lifted.

These controls can be incorporated into a regular <h ref> hyperlink tag, and the default image is also given a 'name' attribute referred to by the onMouse controls, as in this HTML code (note that different utilities create rollover code differently; this is one of the simplest examples):

```
<a href="destination_page.html"
onMouseOver="{button.src='highlighted.gif'; return true}"
onMouseOut=" {button.src='default.gif'; return true}">
onMouseDown=" {button.src='clicked.gif'; return true}">
onMouseUp=" {button.src='default.gif'; return true}">
<img src="default.gif" border="0" name="button"></a>
```

IFRAMES

The <iframe> tag inserts an inline frame into an HTML document. Unlike regular frames, which take up a whole window and which tend to be used for navigation menus or large areas of content, inline frames are effectively small subwindows within pages. They can be used like regular frames and are ideal holders for smaller blocks of text such as dictionary-style definitions, short news items and external images or documents, but also for interactive documents such as quizzes and voting forms.

The <iframe> tag can be used anywhere on an HTML page and, like the <img> tag, can be aligned left, right or centre or assigned to a paragraph to make it stand apart from the rest of the content. The basic tag syntax defines the iframe's name and size and tells the browser to load a page into the frame.

Above: Free code for iframes is available online

Iframe Support

Iframe is only supported by the most recent browsers, and so it is good practice to enter an alternative. This could be a link to an external document, the same text formatted in regular HTML, or a message telling the reader that their browser does not support iframes. This text is inserted inside the <iframe> tag as follows, and will be ignored by browsers that do support iframes:

<iframe src="frame_content.htm" name="content">Sorry, your browser does not support inline frames</iframe>

Size, Spacing and Borders

Like an inline image, the frame can be given dimensions defined in pixels or as a percentage of the parent window. Vertical spacing can also be added around the frame. Iframes cannot be resized like regular frames, but horizontal and vertical scrollbars appear automatically if the framed document is bigger than the frame. By default, the iframe is given a prominent border, but adding border=0 to the <iframe> tag removes this. Matching the background of the frame to that of the framed document will give a seamless effect, and remember that you can define any attribute of the framed document in an attached style sheet.

ADDING LIFE TO PAGES

Many web designers now make use of features such as Flash files to liven up their web pages and bring an extra dimension to the content. Developments are proceeding apace and it is important to keep on top of the latest techniques to keep your pages fresh and up to date.

INCORPORATING FLASH FILES

Once converted from the .fla project format into the browser-compliant .swf movie format, Flash animations are placed on the page using the <object> and <embed> tags. The former defines the size and name of a movie and the version of Flash that was used to create it; the <embed> tag includes its display attributes and the filename and location of the movie.

Your web editor should let you import Flash files just as you would graphics and, in fact, the two elements share common attributes. You can set height, width and alignment, and specify the amount of white space to leave around the object.

Setting Flash Parameters

Flash-specific attributes can be set as parameters. These include background colour – useful if you want your animation or button to blend into its environment – and a quality setting (low quality calls on less processing power to render but obviously degrades the image). Parameters also include the movie's autoplay and loop settings. If autoplay is on, the movie will run as soon as it

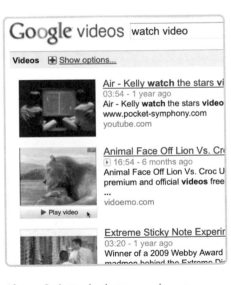

Above: Built–in play buttons make your movies much more accessible

loads (making it essential for buttons and banners). If it is off, the user will have to right-click on the movie and click the Play option. A more user-friendly option would be to build VCR-style play and stop buttons into the original Flash project.

NON-LINEAR ANIMATION

Movement in the form of Flash of GIF animations can catch a web surfer's eye, but will not keep their attention for long if the motion within the animation is monotonous and linear. Real objects rarely move in an absolutely straight line with no regard for the laws of motion or gravity, so why should their animated equivalents? Adding such variation to sequences is termed 'non-linear' animation.

Creating Curving Paths

If a character in an animation – an aeroplane, for instance – moves from one side of the screen to the other in a straight line before bouncing back again, it isn't going to engage the viewer for more than a second or two. The most basic non-linear animation you could add is to run the character through a twisting, curving path. Flash lets you create Bézier curves and run a sprite along the length of the curve with its Motion Guide Tweening feature. Realistically, the plane would also dip and rise as it followed its wavy path, and the Orient to Path Direction option does this by sending an object on its way 'nose first' over the path. Even if you must run an object over a straight line, try twisting it slightly back and forth as it moves for a non-linear, realistic touch.

Too often, objects in animations travel in a straight line at a constant speed. In reality, people accelerate and decelerate as they walk. When an animated object starts moving, let it pick up speed gradually and slow it down before stopping or turning. If you must include a linear, constant, straight-line motion in the middle, keep it as short as possible.

3D Animation

Linearity can be decreased by adding a third dimension to an animation. This need not mean

Above: A fun smoke puff animation at www.gayadesign.com

developing complex 3D graphics, just enlarging or reducing an object gradually to give the impression of it coming towards or moving away from the viewer. This can be combined with shading effects – lightening the sprite as it approaches, darkening as it moves away – to give the impression of it approaching a light source. Similarly, placing an exaggerated light source on a single area of an animation prevents linearity with a simple twist.

NON-LINEAR DESIGN

There can be a tendency, particularly in table-based page design, to use sharp, positive delineation between areas of a web page – a big horizontal block for a header, a solid rectangular menu on the left and the main content area sliced up like a Neapolitan ice cream. While this may seem orderly, on a subconscious level, it is far from engaging and, by adding non-linear elements such as curved lines and patterns, you can eliminate the impression of an austere grid and draw the user in towards the more important parts of the site.

Curved Underlines

Rather than separating the header from the rest of the page with a sharp horizontal line, divide the elements using a slight wave using your graphic package's Bézier curve tool and apply a gentle drop shadow. This gives the impression of three-dimensional non-linearity by making it look as though the header is sitting slightly above the flat surface of the page. The same effect works by dividing left-hand menu bars from the main content area with a vertical curve. You can combine the two using a framed effect, where the content area sits in a round-edged panel shadowed or bevelled to sit above or below a coloured frame which unites the header and the menu.

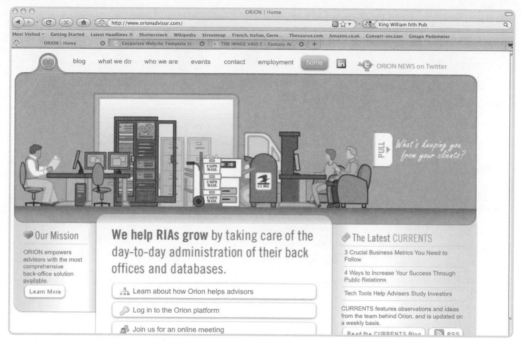

Above: Rounded corners and curves soften the impression of a website

Guiding the Eye

Curves can be used to guide the reader's eye towards the most important element of the page by using a deeper curve as a gentle but persuasive pointing device. Remember to contrast the colour of the menu or header with the page background for increased effectiveness.

DESIGNING A 3D INTERFACE

Although the computer screen is a two-dimensional medium, web graphics software packages make it easy to create an impression of depth to apply a pseudo-3D appearance. Using a few simple tricks, you could make your site stand out and give it a professional touch. Most of these effects can be created in image-editing programs such as Adobe's Fireworks or Photoshop's ImageReady utility and Corel's specialist web design applications.

Adding Shadows

In the real, three-dimensional world, light sources cast shadows on to background objects, so adding shadows and lighting effects to a page can create the impression of three dimensions. Placing a drop shadow behind an image – whether it is a cutout, a button or a geometric shape – lifts that element off the page. If you use more than one drop shadow on the same page, keep the angle and depth of the shadow constant to suggest a regular light source; shadows slanting in different directions will look unnatural.

Above: Just some of the more simple effects you can achieve to contribute to a 3D interface

Inner Shadows

Some programs let you add inner shadows as easily as you can add drop shadows. Inner shadows usually sit inside geometric shapes and give them a sunken effect, raising the main body of the page to the foreground. Unlike drop shadows, inner shadows point towards the light source. Again, if you combine inner and drop shadows on a page, keep the angle of the light source consistent. Inner shadows can be added to large white-out text headlines and banners. This creates the impression that the headline or logo has been cut out of the foreground, and works best on black or dark-coloured backgrounds.

Motion Blur

Motion blur is a form of exaggerated shadow to suggest movement as well as depth. Used sparingly, it can add additional depth to a page. It can be combined with animated graphics in order to suggest that an item is moving towards the reader. This can be created simply by enlarging and shrinking the main character in an animation as it moves, to give the impression of it approaching.

Embossing

Embossing tools use subtle shading effects to make elements such as buttons appear to sink into or raise out of their surroundings. You can apply an inset or a raised emboss effect. This works well when lifting headline text gently out of its background. Embossing works particularly well when the embossed image and its background are the same colour. This can give the effect of embossed paper or, with a light grey tint on the background and the foreground, of a stamped metal panel.

Textures

Textures, combined with colour and lighting, can be used to enhance the appearance of embossed elements. Brown-tinted embossed text or line-art on a wooden texture can look like a carving, while a metal textured image can resemble a coin or engraved metal nameplate. Dedicated 3D-graphics utilities let you add a light source and light type such as spot, point or distance to enhance this effect, and tutorials at sites such as Web Design Library (www.webdesign.org) can help you get the best out of the myriad effects and techniques available.

Above: Online tutorials can help when using textures

Bevelling

Bevelling (*see also* pages 142–43) adds raised edges to buttons and other small geometric shapes. An automatic inner bevel applies a raised and textured border to the inside of the button, while the outer bevel adds an additional border to the button. The size of the border, inside or out, can be set by the user but, on smaller buttons, keep it small or there will be more bevel than button. Fireworks offers several styles so you can apply a smooth bevel, emulate convex or concave slopes, or create a frame which indents the content of the centre of the button.

CREATING A BUSINESS WEBSITE

An Internet presence is now a crucial part of corporate strategy. Websites can be used for advertising or promotion, as a sales medium or as a conduit for contact between the firm and its customers or partners. The line of business will largely determine the website's content and structure.

KEY ELEMENTS AND STEPS

Wholesale and retail sales lend themselves perfectly to e-commerce, while more abstract business-to-business service providers might prefer to advertise their wares online as a gateway to conventional dealings. When planning your business site, think carefully not only about the design, but also the content – write this in a word-processing package first and get someone to proofread it before you put any of the information on your site.

→ **Programs**: Use high-end web editors such as Adobe Dreamweaver to ease collaboration on sites, and simplify site management across a number of machines. Complement the web editor with a web-specific graphics package such as Photoshop or Fireworks.

→ **About Us**: Every company site should include an overview of the firm; an 'About Us' section can provide a description of the core activities of the company, a brief history and details of where it is based or where its headquarters and any satellite offices are. Senior personnel should be profiled, and an organization chart added to show the hierarchical structure of staff and departments.

→ **Contact details**: While you can simply publish the email address of every member of staff, visitors might choose a recipient for their message at random and it might not be dealt with at all, losing valuable business and damaging a firm's reputation. Instead, incorporate an online form and direct its contents towards a central distributor – an office secretary, for instance – who can forward the query to the most suitable party and follow up to ensure that prompt action is taken.

Site map: Add a site map, which should list every page under each section heading, so that users can access a page quickly and easily.

House style: Much of the design of business sites will be determined by the company's own house style. The colour scheme, for instance, may be based on the existing masthead, and the logo may be simple enough to use online. However, if a logo is too involved or a colour scheme is old fashioned, a venture on to the Internet is the perfect opportunity for a revamp of a company's brand and image.

Product display: If you are setting up an e-commerce section, do not cram all your products on to a single page. Instead, position them three or four to a page or use e-commerce software with a search facility.

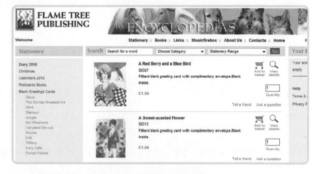

Secure transactions: E-commerce service providers and ISPs sometimes provide credit card authorization tools

Above: Make it easy to find and purchase your products

so that users can buy online easily and safely; the companies that offer this service usually take a cut of each transaction, but it is worth it for a secure validation system.

Professional quality: Do not cut corners when choosing a firm to host your site. Free web space is an unprofessional no-no, and regular consumer accounts are unlikely to offer the stability required for a successful site. Find a reliable corporate account and sign up to a service level agreement that guarantees maximum uptime. Server problems could damage customer confidence and cost you sales.

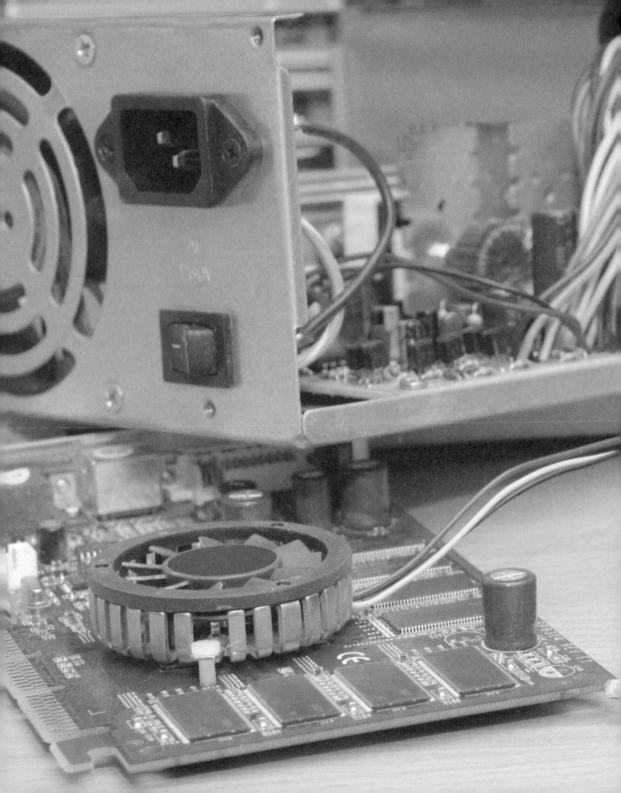

TECHNICAL MATTERS

LANGUAGES & GETTING ROUND THEM

Throughout this book, several different programming languages have been referred to. This section explains the differences between them and which one should be used for which application. Of course, you may have contributors who have no knowledge of web languages – in this case, content management systems (CMS) are used to enable people to upload their material to the website.

XML

Extensible Markup Language. Although this is similar to HTML (*see* pages 28–29) in syntax, it operates differently. While HTML controls how documents are displayed, XML simply looks at the structure. It separates the content on a page from the way it is presented. As a markup language, HTML uses a fixed number of tags. It also specifies exactly what each one means and how it will look in the browser. XML only uses the tags to separate pieces of data. Thus, <p> in an XML file is not necessarily a paragraph mark, but can be anything – such as price or person – according to the application that reads it.

With XML, users create their own tags for special kinds of documents, such as a medical chart or a transcript of a play; hence it is extensible. XML-capable browsers then lay out the document following instructions supplied in the associated style sheets.

Above: XML code

XHTML

Markup Language. As the next generation of HTML, XHTML is a much tougher taskmaster specifically designed for smaller handheld devices. As demands on browsers are becoming more complicated, so the software gets bigger. This means they are not always suitable for smaller devices, such as handhelds. EXtensible Hypertext Markup Language (XHTML) aims to cut HTML down in size by simplifying the rules and being much stricter about applying them. It also introduces a new idea of profiles, by which not all devices support all tags. With Modularized XHTML, devices like PDAs can say what tags they do or do not support (e.g. not colour) while websites let them know what tags are needed.

XML Generations

XHTML is often seen as the next generation of HTML. It is based on the latest HTML standard, version 4.01, and is designed to be used with XML. While it might not always seem so, HTML is generally forgiving if you make a mistake, such as improperly nesting a tag.

DHTML

Dynamic Hypertext Markup Language. The aim of Dynamic HTML (DHTML) is to take the ordinary text-and-graphics web page and bring it to life. Using DHTML, content on the page can change and images and text can move, appear, disappear or change style as wanted. What is more, all the coding is in the client-side, so there are no delays with requests going to and from the web server.

Technology Mix

In fact, DHTML is not a single identifiable product in the way JavaScript is. Instead, it is a combination of technologies, including HTML, JavaScript and CSS, that enables designers to control each element on the page. In effect, it allows you to hide or show objects and move them around, by changing the CSS positioning properties. No plug-ins are required and files are small as they are text files, which are quicker to download than graphics files, and render faster than alternatives such as Flash. The main fly in the ointment is the variable support for DHTML among the different types of browser. Although there are workarounds, it is not yet totally cross-browser compatible.

JAVA

Java was originally designed as a programming language and operating system for the consumer electronics market, to control everything from TV sets to toasters. Although it did not succeed there, it had a number of features which made it ideal for the Web. It is small (as it was designed to fit into items with little memory), can be transferred quickly and is platform-independent.

Above: You can download Java from the Java website

An Interpreted Language

It is now essential in web design, and achieves this by being an interpreted rather than a compiled language. Unlike C++ – on which it is based – it is not compiled into code for a specific platform, such as the PC; instead, it is put into a single compiled version called Java bytecode. On the Web, this is interpreted by a virtual machine, usually running within the browser, on whichever platform is being used.

Applets

Although it is a fully fledged programming language, Java is mainly used on the Web to create applets – which can be embedded on a page. These programs, which have the extension .class, can add all sorts of interactive features to a site, as well as enable multimedia animations and database integration.

ACTIVEX CONTROLS

ActiveX controls can add greater interactivity to web pages than other technologies, but you should bear in mind that they also carry greater risks. ActiveX is the brand name of a group of technologies developed by Microsoft, which sets down rules for how applications share information. ActiveX programs – called controls – are reusable bits of software that add interactivity to a web page. Though ActiveX is not actually a language, it is discussed here because these mini programs are similar to Java applets. They can be as complex as a video player or as simple as a highlighting button.

The controls are downloaded to your hard drive, where they are saved; this means that, if you visit a page which needs the same control, it will not be downloaded again. This is the notable advantage of ActiveX over Java applets, which are not cached and have to be downloaded each time you visit a page. Once downloaded, ActiveX controls can access all parts of your computer. Consequently, they carry a greater security risk than Java applets, which only interact with your machine within a specified area (sandbox). Accordingly, you can set different levels of security within your browser, to warn you every time an ActiveX control is encountered.

JAVASCRIPT

Client-side scripting language that can add animation and interactive effects to websites without demanding the programming skills of server-side programs. Despite the name, JavaScript is not related to Java. Originally developed for Netscape's Navigator Browser, it is a client-side scripting language designed to bring some basic interactivity to web pages. It enables designers to control different elements.

Scripting-programming Language

A scripting language such as JavaScript is somewhere between a markup language, such as HTML, and a fully-fledged programming language, such as Java. The advantage of JavaScript is that it requires few programming skills. Basic animation and special effects can be added to web pages without the complication of server-side programming such as CGI.

Integration

The extra functionality JavaScript supplies is added through short snippets of code that are written directly within the HTML code on a web page. It is enclosed within the <script> tag to tell the browser to run it as a JavaScript program. <script> tags are most commonly put in the <head> section, as it means the script can start running

Above: Javascript offers useful ways to present image galleries

while the rest of the page is downloading. However, scripts that write text to the screen or HTML are usually best placed within the <body> section.

You do not have to write your own JavaScript at all. There are programs, such as Adobe's Dreamweaver, which do the coding for you, adding their built-in 'behaviors' (JavaScript) to the HTML. There are also sites where you can freely download scripts to add to your page, such as the JavaScript source (www.javascriptsource.com). However, as it runs on the client, JavaScript does need to be supported by the browser. Unfortunately, not only do different browsers interpret JavaScript in different ways, but so do different versions of the same browser. If there is a script on your page that the browser does not understand, it will be interpreted as straight text and look strange on screen, or worse – generate an error message and crash the user's browser.

PERL

Not as flawless as its name suggests, Perl stands for Practical Extraction and Report Language. Because it is good at processing text, it has become one of the most popular languages for writing CGI scripts, particularly on UNIX machines. It has the advantage over CGI programs written in other languages, such as C or C++, in that it does not need to be compiled, which makes it easier to debug, modify and maintain.

Ready-made Scripts

While you would need programming experience to write a Perl script from scratch, there are plenty of ready-made scripts available. They include scripts to help process forms and send their contents as emails. Many web-hosting companies have a set of standard scripts already installed that you can use simply by linking to them. Others allow you to upload your own. There are also archives on the Web, such as http://www.scripts.com/perl-scripts/. Even so, it is important to follow any instructions that come with it. As Perl is an interpreted language, make sure there is a Perl interpreter installed on the server to enable the script to work. You will also need to know the exact pathname to the script.

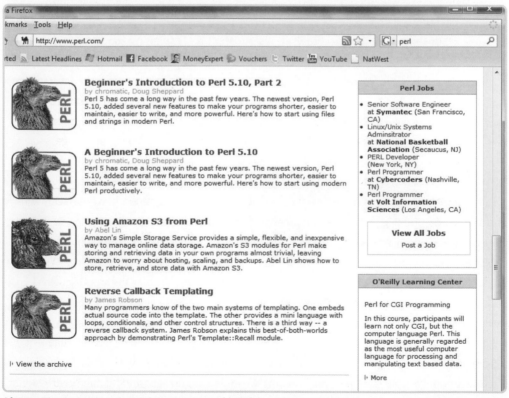

Above: The Perl website provides an archive of helpful articles on using Perl

VBSCRIPT

VBScript is short for Visual Basic Script Edition. It is a client-side scripting language, similar to JavaScript, and it is embedded in the HTML file that uses it. By being inserted in the <head> of the document, the script is loaded into the memory while the rest of the page is downloading. The script will run as it is read – if, for example, it is checking which version of a browser is being used – or on some event, such as a click of the mouse or a rollover.

Dynamic Content

VBScript is based on Microsoft's Visual Basic programming language, although it is simpler to use. It allows web designers to provide dynamic content to their pages, including interactive navigational controls. VBScript is supported by Microsoft's Internet Explorer browser, but not by Firefox. Similarly, most modern browsers' users can turn off scripting support as a security measure. Because there are no guarantees that the client-side scripting is supported, it is advisable to provide alternative content between the <noscript> and </noscript> tags. One way round this is to use VBScript as a server-side scripting language and it is the default language for ASP (Active Server Pages).

CMS

This is not a web language but, rather, a way of avoiding knowing one. Good writers with equally good web programming skills are a rare breed, so online publishers and other companies where a lot of people produce a lot of pages for the same site use a content management system (CMS) to upload words and pictures. Oddly, no one content management system dominates the market in the way Photoshop rules image editing and Microsoft Word is the standard word processor. Companies often have their CMS custom-built but, in recent years, web content management systems have been made available online for personal and corporate use.

Joomla!

The most popular CMS is Joomla! (joomla.org), which lets you create and manage professional-looking websites using a simple interface not dissimilar from the forms-based blog front-end.

You will need to download the Joomla! software, upload it to your server and link it to a database (this is a straightforward step-by-step process).

Once you have created your system of sections and menu items (and this structure should be set out in advance just like a home-coded site), a wide community of developers is constantly developing plug-in modules, such as polls and galleries, that you can add to your site (some charge, others are free). The same community is usually on hand to answer your queries on any aspect of the system. Designers are also hard at work creating templates of all colours and styles for you to incorporate into your site.

Others

Some users might find Joomla! a little difficult to install and use, but other CMS packages are available, such as the self-explanatory CMS Made Simple (http://www.cmsmadesimple.org/). Most good CMS packages will also help your site's searchability with Google-friendly URLs and correctly assigned <meta> tags.

Above: The Joomla! content management system

SERVER-SIDE TECHNOLOGY

Server-side technology is what makes your pages dynamic and allows you to respond to your clients' access needs. Understanding the technology is therefore key to successful relationships with your users.

ASP

Microsoft's framework for server-side scripting can handle major e-commerce sites or simple form-processing for those working with Windows-based web servers. It can be used to construct major e-commerce websites but is also useful for anyone with a Windows-based web server. ASP (Active Server Pages) enables you to process and store information – such as from a form – in a database. It also allows you to personalize content according to users' preferences, or to vary the web page layout for different browsers.

How ASP Works

ASP pages usually have the extension .asp instead of .html. This indicates that it is a text file with HTML and scripting (usually, it is written in VBScript). When your browser requests an .asp file from the server, the web server calls ASP, which processes the file from top to bottom and runs any scripts commands before sending the results as a web page to the browser. As the scripts run on the server rather than the client, the process is faster than client-side processing. In addition, scripts cannot easily be copied, as the commands used to create the page run server-side and are not viewable within the page they generate.

CGI

CGI (Common Gateway Interface) is a simple standard for linking programs and web servers, to provide server-side processing to websites. It is a simple protocol for communication between a web server and an external program. CGI handles the flow of information between the two, in the same way as HTTP regulates the transfer of data between the server and the browser.

Scripts

CGI applications, sometimes called scripts, work in a different way. They receive the data from the server and return it via the Common Gateway Interface. These programs are the most popular way for users to interact dynamically with the site – such as connecting to a database, sending information via email or processing information from a form. They can be written in any programming language, but are typically in C, C++, Perl, AppleScript or Visual Basic.

```
guestbook - WordPad
File  Edit  View  Insert  Format  Help

#!/usr/bin/perl
# $Id: guestbook.pl,v 1.1 2004/04/13 04:15:36 morpheus Exp $
# guestbook -- demo program demonstrating CGI.pm and other
functionality.

use strict;

use CGI qw(:all);        # import shortcuts
use Fcntl qw(:flock);    # imports LOCK_EX, LOCK_SH, LOCK_NB

sub bail {
  my $error = "@_";
  print h2("Unexpected Error"), p($error), end_html;
  die $error;
}

my (
        $CHATNAME, # name of guestbook file
        $MAXSAVE,  # how many to keep
        $TITLE,    # page title & header
        $cur,      # new entry in the guestbook
        @entries,  # all cur entries
        $entry,    # one particular entry
);

$TITLE = "My Nifty Guestbook";
```

Above: CGI Script

JSP

JHTML was the earlier method for including a Java program as part of a web page, but that was replaced by JavaServer Pages (JSP). This is a server-side technology that, together with Java servlets, which bring dynamic content to the Web, were developed by Sun as an alternative to Microsoft's Active Server Pages (ASP).

The advantage of JSP pages is that they separate the static HTML elements on the page – the actual design and display of the page – from the dynamically generated HTML. JSP technology has the advantage over pure server-side applications such as CGI in that it does not generate the entire page each time, even when most of it is the same. As a result, designers can change the look and feel of the page without compromising any of the back-end coding. They simply leave places where servlet programmers can insert the dynamic content.

SOFTWARE

SOFTWARE GIANTS

The two leaders on web-design software are Microsoft and Adobe. Getting to grips with the range of software they offer will help you choose the one that is right for you.

MICROSOFT

Microsoft is without doubt the biggest desktop software company on Earth and, after a slow start in web software, its Internet Explorer is now the dominant browser, and the accompanying Outlook is the de facto standard email tool. Microsoft also produces software to manage the servers that many websites sit on, and the Windows operating systems are fully Internet-enabled. Through a massive process of acquisition and development, Microsoft has also come to offer many of the Web's most popular services, including the Hotmail email service and the Bing search engine.

Above: Microsoft's Bing search engine

ADOBE

The long-time favourite developer of the design community, Adobe eased its proponents' journey to the Internet by adding web-specific features to its set of established design programs, which it markets in two web-specific editions of its Creative Suite (CS) software collection. The first, CS Web Standard, contains the web page and image-creation tools that Adobe acquired from Macromedia – Dreamweaver (website creation and layout), Fireworks (image creation and editing), Flash (for animation and interactivity) and Contribute (a content management interface for Dreamweaver).

Web Premium

CS Web Premium is a high-end edition for professional graphic designers, adding the image editing package Photoshop and Adobe's vector-based drawing application, Illustrator, into the mix.

Acrobat

Cross-platform document writer and reader. Adobe's Acrobat lets publishers distribute documents originally created for print-based publication over the Web, without compromising the design and without relying on the recipient having a copy of the software application that created the original.

Documents created in common office applications such as Word, Excel or PowerPoint or desktop-publishing programs such as InDesign can be converted into Adobe's portable document format (PDF) using Acrobat. Anyone with a copy of Adobe Reader, available free from www.adobe.com, can view the file. Browsers will open a hyperlinked PDF file within the main browser window just like any other web page. Files can be saved to the hard disk and printed, and documents can be read on Windows and Macintosh computers. Because it compresses large documents into convenient, platform-independent files, Acrobat is commonly used to distribute longer, design-led publications such as company reports or brochures. Acrobat users can also create interactive online application forms, called eForms, which recipients can complete and return using their browsers; interactive buttons and web links can be added to Acrobat files; and the text in the documents is fully searchable. Users of the full Acrobat program can add comments and virtual sticky notes to a PDF file of a draft document using a browser.

WEB EDITING

These are the places to begin – the all–singing, all–dancing software packages to get you started on designing and creating your website.

DREAMWEAVER (ADOBE)

Adobe's web editor Dreamweaver lies at the heart of a website production system that includes the dominant multimedia standards Flash and Shockwave. Dreamweaver is a favourite with professional web designers, but can cater for users of all degrees of experience.

Web-page Creation

The program offers several ways to create a web page. Designers can sketch a design for a site in a graphics package and then trace table elements, text areas and images over it. This way, they can output to a regular page, or to the layers-based format, which ensures pixel-perfect design in the latest browsers. Alternatively, you can create your pages in Dreamweaver's WYSIWYG (*see page 29*) display window, entering text and adding other elements from images to animations and applets. A tabbed window also gives access to the HTML source, should you want to check why an effect is not working as it should. The program will also check your HTML for errors and compatibility with all the latest and old versions of browsers.

HTML Styles

Site-wide consistency can be achieved using Dreamweaver's HTML styles. Styles let you save a set of attributes which can be assigned to characters or a paragraph with a single click. Dreamweaver then applies all the correct HTML codes to the text for you. A more efficient option is to use cascading style sheets (CSS), for which Dreamweaver has full support. The program also supports Java and ActiveX items, and Flash animations and graphics are linked dynamically to Flash and Fireworks respectively.

Dreamweaver boasts impressive site control features. You can view your entire site as a conventional Windows/Mac directory or as a tree structure. FTP links can be established to a remote server and updated pages uploaded automatically. If a group of colleagues will be editing the content of your site's pages, they can add comments to any elements they have worked on for future reference.

FREEWAY PRO (SOFTPRESS)

SoftPress Freeway Pro is a rarity among web editors, as it does not require any understanding of HTML and is not constrained by the limitations of the Web. Freeway – available for the Macintosh only, for around £150 – provides an easy route from page design to the Web, as its interface is based on a desktop publishing metaphor, right down to the keyboard shortcuts. Designers can lay out pages as they would in InDesign or QuarkXPress, and Freeway will export all the code and graphics for publication. Users can view and edit the HTML code as they work, but they should not have to, as the HTML export adheres tightly to standards, with options to write HTML 3.2, HTML 3.2 with cascading style sheets, HTML 4.0 and XHTML 1.0

Image Processing

Built-in image processing means you can import layered Photoshop files, PICTs (a Mac graphics file format) and TIFFs, position them in regular or custom frames and Freeway will export them as GIFs or JPEGs. Flash and QuickTime movies are supported, and text can be saved as graphics. Rollovers and image maps can be applied. Users can write or import third-party code such as JavaScript pop-up menus or controllers for importing database content, and Freeway can create a visual map of a site's links to ease navigation. Plug-ins can also be incorporated to add interactive features such as an online store, and Freeway Pro 5 now supports site development for the Apple iPhone.

GRAPHICS, IMAGE EDITING AND ANIMATION

Adobe's range of image–editing software is the market leader, but Corel has some features that can come in handy when creating your website.

FIREWORKS (ADOBE)

The web graphics weapon in Adobe's web arsenal is Fireworks, an easy-to-use program which lets web newcomers and professional designers create optimized, high-quality graphics with ease. Its primary role is for creating simple vector graphics such as buttons, dynamic elements like rollovers and animated GIFs, and optimizing images for publication on the Web. With this in mind, Adobe has kept the interface – and the feature set – it acquired from Fireworks' original publisher Macromedia straightforward but powerful.

ILLUSTRATOR (ADOBE)

As well as conventional vector drawing tools, Illustrator has adopted many traditionally bitmap-only tools from Photoshop. The program supports Photoshop's extensive range of filters and plug-ins, and boasts a range of freestyle brushes normally only found in bitmap graphics software. Tools for liquifying objects and applying lens flares are new additions, and layered designs literally add another dimension to Illustrator's vector capabilities. The program's layer masks are fully exportable to Photoshop.

PHOTOSHOP (ADOBE)

The Photoshop interface consists of a toolbox and a collection of tabbed context-sensitive dialog boxes that control the attributes of each tool. Brush, airbrush and pencil tools are available to create new bitmap images, and editing tools such as burn, smudge and sharpen can be applied to selected areas of imported or scanned images. As well as the usual brightness, contrast and colour adjusting filters, an ever-expanding range of art and special effects (warps, radial blurs and a liquify command) can transform images into professional compositions for print or the Web.

All images are created as a series of layers, so that different elements of a composition can be edited separately and 'flattened' into a single layer shortly before exporting to a publishable format. Text elements sit on separate layers, and paragraph styles can be applied to each block of text.

Photoshop.com

Photoshop.com is the online edition of Adobe's high-end image editing software. It does not have the high-end features of the full application, but it is ideal for making the kinds of changes you need to prepare an image for your website. Sign up for an Adobe account and upload your photo and you can crop and rotate it, change the white balance, sharpen an image or add soft focus, remove red-eye or add distortion effects. You can preview all your changes before committing and, when you are done, save your photo back to your hard drive to upload to your website. A very handy site if you are away from your image editor.

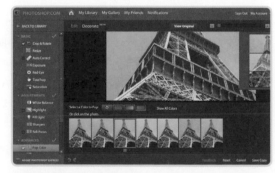

Above: The potential results of your editing are shown in thumbnails along the bottom of the Photoshop.com work area

CORELDRAW

The Corel Corporation's graphic design package is now almost 20 years old and has kept pace with the times with the addition of web-specific features as well as the latest image-editing tools. The CorelDraw vector imaging product now comes as part of the CorelDraw Graphics Suite, along with image editor Photo-Paint and bitmap-to-vector tracing tool PowerTrace.

PAINT SHOP PRO

PSP has a good selection of textures and gradient fills, and its Picture Tube tool lets you paint with patterns and import a gallery of clip-art images into your designs. It also boasts special enhanced filters for cleaning up photos – tools such as the red-eye remover will prove useful to webmasters whose sites feature regular photo galleries, and the Smart Photo Fix instantly corrects lighting and colour problems with automated tools. Blurred pictures can also be sharpened automatically.

ANIMATION WITH FLASH

Adobe's Flash has become the industry standard for low-bandwidth interactive animations, presentations and even applications over the Web. The Flash program, currently part of Adobe's CS4 suite, lets designers create content for distribution to, according to Adobe, more than 99 per cent of the world's PCs that currently run the Flash Player.

As part of Adobe's powerful arsenal of Internet tools, Flash integrates tightly with its siblings, particularly the Dreamweaver web editor and Illustrator vector graphics package. Elements can be imported seamlessly from one package to another and back again for re-editing, and interactive buttons, text elements and drop-down menu styles can be created in Flash and configured to suit a specific page or site in Dreamweaver. Because Flash objects (or symbols) are scalable, they can be imported into Dreamweaver and enlarged or reduced with no loss of quality.

Flash Components

The basic Flash interface consists of the Timeline, the main 'Stage' window and a series of tabbed toolbars and palettes. The stage shows how the Flash window would look at a given time in the animation, and scrolling along the Timeline allows you to move elements and set objects accordingly. Simple animations are straightforward, thanks to Flash's Tweening tools. Short for 'inbetweening', these let the user set starting and finishing points for an object and calculates the movement, morphing pattern or colour changes in between. Audio clips, bitmap images and digital movies can also be built into sequences.

As well as diverting animations, Flash can be used to create powerful interactive web applications using Adobe's ActionScript, which has the same structure and syntax as JavaScript but which can be authored graphically in Flash. The software also offers connectivity to databases and middleware applications via standard XML protocols.

Flash Player

Plug-in for playing Flash animations. Flash has become the industry standard for low-bandwidth, interactive scalable animations, and browser developers acknowledge this by adding Adobe's Flash Player to their latest releases. Standalone streaming video players like RealPlayer and QuickTime can also play Flash content.

Flash Player is essentially a plug-in that integrates seamlessly with a browser to play any Flash content included in a web page. Content created using the current version of Flash can be viewed on more than 99 per cent of the world's PCs.

Updates

The Flash Player is reasonably backwards-compatible, so content created using Flash version 5 could be played on the latest Flash Player. However, to play the latest Flash content, the latest player is required. Fortunately for users and content providers, if the correct version is not detected, the latest edition (weighing in at around 50 KB) will be downloaded free of charge and installed seamlessly. Alternatively, users can download the Player themselves from

Above: Adobe Flash installed

www.adobe.com/flashplayer/. Adobe makes tweaks, enhancements and bug fixes to the Player every few months so, if you are a developer, sign up to receive regular news and updates from the software company.

WEB BROWSING

Although there are hundreds of browsers available, a handful of them have the market cornered – these are the most familiar names that aid you in your Internet searches.

INTERNET EXPLORER (MICROSOFT)

Set at the heart of the Windows operating system, Microsoft Internet Explorer (IE) is the most widely used browser on the Internet today. The software is available to download free from www.microsoft.com/windows/ie.

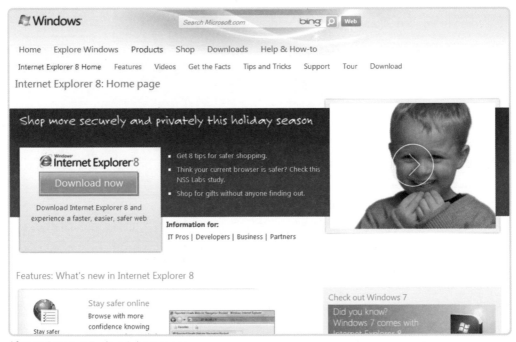

Above: Internet Explorer's homepage

Browser technology has slowed down since constant changes to HTML competition between Microsoft and Netscape led to a rapid series of updates in the mid-1990s. Subsequent updates have concentrated on the experience of browsing, and the latest version – version 8 – is no exception.

Standard Support

On the technical side, the latest HTML, Ajax and CSS standards are supported, along with support for Accelerators, which allow supported web applications to be invoked without explicitly navigating to them, and WebSlices, which allow portions of pages to be subscribed to and monitored from a redesigned favourites bar. Other features include InPrivate privacy enhancements and the SmartScreen phishing filter. Extras include email and newsgroup software Outlook Express and Adobe's Flash Player.

MOZILLA FIREFOX

Mozilla Firefox is the second most popular browser in terms of usage on the Internet. It is credited with popularizing the tabbed browsing that is now common to all browsers and, unlike Microsoft's Internet Explorer, runs across several platforms, including various versions of Mac OS X, Microsoft Windows, Linux, and many other Unix-like operating systems.

GOOGLE CHROME

Google Chrome is a web browser published by Google for Windows in December 2008, with development versions of Chrome for Linux and Mac OS X following in June 2009. Chrome – Internet service giant Google's first foray into desktop software – is claimed to be faster and more secure and stable than other browsers. Since its launch it has been joined by Google's Chrome OS, an operating system dedicated to running only programs over the Internet, such as the Google Apps suite of email, word processor, spreadsheet and calendar applications.

FURTHER READING

Beaird, Jason, *The Principles of Beautiful Web Design*, Sitepoint, 2007

Cederholm, Dan, *Bulletproof Web Design: Improving Flexibility and Protecting Against Worst-Case Scenarios with XHTML and CSS*, New Riders, 2007

Chapman, Nigel, *Web Design: A Complete Introduction*, John Wiley, 2006

Grappone, Jennifer, *Search Engine Optimization: An Hour a Day*, John Wiley, 2008

Lloyd, Ian, *Build Your Own Website the Right Way Using HTML and CSS*, Sitepoint, 2008
Lopuck, Lisa, *Web Design for Dummies*, John Wiley, 2006

MacDonald, Matthew, *Creating a Web Site: The Missing Manual*, Pogue Press, 2009
MacRea, Kyle, *Build Your Own Website*, J. H. Haynes & Co, 2009

McIntire, Penny, *Visual Design for the Modern Web*, New Riders, 2007

McNeill, Patrick, *The Web Designer's Idea Book*, HOW Books, 2008

Quick, Richard, *Web Design in Easy Steps*, In Easy Steps Ltd, 2010

Robbins, Jennifer Niederst, *Web Design: A Beginner's Guide to (X)HTML, Style Sheets and Web Graphics*, O'Reilly Media, 2009

Shea, David and Holzschlag, Molly, *The Zen of CSS Design: Visual Enlightenment for the Web*, Peachpit Press, 2005

Smith, Jon, *Get Into Bed With Google: Top Ranking Search Optimisation Techniques*, Infinite Ideas Ltd, 2008

Thomson, Philip, *Website Essentials: A Guide to Planning, Designing and Managing Your Website*, Frogeye Publications, 2006

Wiedemann, Julius, *Web Design: Flash Sites*, Taschen, 2006

Wiedemann, Julius, *Web Design: E-commerce*, Taschen, 2006

WEBSITES

This is just a selection of some of the many useful websites that can offer all manner of help in designing and creating your own website.

Web Hosting

www.angelfire.com

Part of the giant Lycos network, this is a personal website builder that offers free graphics, template designs and a personalized URL. The easy-to-use building tools provide access to cut-and-paste JavaScript and CGI scripts and the service also supports sites created in Microsoft's FrontPage. The only drawback is that the free service places ads on your site; however, you get a reasonable 20 MB of space and free games that you can add to your web page.

www.tripod.com

As with any homepage hosting service, Tripod offer a range of schemes, from the ad-supported basic free site to a subscription-based service minus the banner ads. Part of the giant Lycos network, the monthly paid-for web-hosting services enable you to add more disk space and bandwidth.

Tutorials

www.w3schools.com

Novice or expert, there is something for everyone at W3Schools, whether it is a reference guide, online validation or a step-by-step. W3Schools.com certainly packs a great deal of information into a relatively short space. It caters for both the learner and the advanced.

www.killersites.com

Although visitors to this site would benefit from reading the book it is linked to (*Creating Killer Websites* by David Siegel), it can stand by itself. Established as a backup to the book and featuring some of the example sites used in the book, KillerSites has become a multimedia treasure trove, featuring video tutorials on web design and programming techniques.

www.webreference.com

A reference site mainly for those with some experience of web design and development, Webreference.com does have links that are useful for everyone. Its tutorials and articles deal with the latest cutting edge technology, rather than basic 'how to' guides. The expert comment covers 3D, Graphics and Design, HTML, DHTML and JavaScript as well as Perl and XML.

www.htmlgoodies.com

HTML Goodies has HTML tutorials a-plenty, going from the basic primer for beginners through to a full list of the HTML tags and more advanced techniques. But along with these is a series of primers and reference pieces on all the topics the aspiring web designer and developer needs to know, including a guide to server error codes and a discussion on when to use databases.

Images

www.clipart-graphics.net

This site is a kind of graphics co-operative. It does not hold any free clip art itself, but instead it links through to a host of sites that do – some 290 sites at the last count. It ranks those sites in order of the amount of traffic they bring to the main directory site. Alongside each entry in the directory is a measure of the traffic flow, so you can see which sites are proving popular.

www.freeimages.co.uk

Most stock photo libraries will offer free images as a taster for their commercial offerings, but this offers free web-quality images as long as you register – they make their money selling high-resolution images for print publication.

www.corbis.com

While CorbisImages' online gallery has more than two million images, this is still not the full picture: the total Corbis collection numbers some 65 million images. Traditionally licensed images and royalty-free pictures can be bought and downloaded online. The searchable online catalogue covers celebrities, sports icons, famous photographers, fine art and more.

www.gettyimages.com

Getty Images now own a number of famous photo libraries, including the Image Bank, Stone and the Hulton Archive with its unique collection of pictures of historic figures. For designers, the centre of this library of millions of images is the 'Images' section, which is split into 'Creative' and 'Editorial' categories.

Fonts

www.fontseek.com

Fontseek is a search engine that can access more than 55,000 fonts in its database, commercial and freeware. Despite the fact that there are only a handful of fonts that most browsers are able to recognize – or that we can safely assume users have on their machine – there are many thousands more available online.

www.1001freefonts.com

If you decide you want a decorative font to use in logos etc., there are plenty of free fonts for either the PC or Mac at this site.

Useful Linking Sites

www.youtube.com

For webmasters, YouTube has taken the pain and expense out of incorporating video into their own websites. Because YouTube videos are essentially displayed in a Flash animation, you can add any video you find on YouTube to your site simply by copying the code from the 'Embed' field to the right of the video and pasting in into the HTML view of your web editor.

http://maps.google.uk

Want to show people where your office, shop, club or party is? Rather than pasting a badly scanned page of the *A to Z* into your website, why not add a Google Map? This will not only point out your visitors' destination with a big red arrow, but also let them zoom in and out to examine their route or view it as a map or a satellite photo.

http://stores.shop.ebay.co.uk

If you are a small business or cottage industry, e-commerce systems can be difficult to install and maintain, and dealing with credit card transactions can be expensive and fraught with security issues. A cost-effective solution is to open a shop on Auction website eBay. For a small monthly subscription, you can sell your wares to eBay customers, have your shop listed by category, modify your shop to use a similar colour scheme to your regular site and manage your earnings through an associated PayPal account.

Other Useful Sites

www.w3.org

Since its inception in 1994, W3C has set the standards for HTML and set recommended practices in order to try to ensure the openness of the Web. W3C is also a forum for new developments. A lot of information can be found at their website www.w3.org. Not only does it cover the history and future of the Web, but it also enables you to test the validity of your code and to look up definitions for various tags and attributes.

www.net2ftp.com

If you have ever wanted to update a website but been away from your PC, net2ftp is for you. Rather than using an FTP client such as CuteFTP, net2ftp lets you access your web servers directly from the Internet. Just enter your FTP server name, username and password and you will be logged in. You can even edit pages through the browser, so there is no need to download the files to a shared PC for someone else to stumble across.

www.response-o-matic.com

Online form-processing services such as Response-O-Matic enable you to add interactive forms to your site without doing any programming. The basic forms for your site are designed in HTML. The questions can be what you like and the forms can use any combination you wish of check boxes, radio buttons and drop-down menus. To ease the process, you can create a form template, using the Form Wizard, and then just modify the questions to the ones you want.

INDEX